DEMOCRACY IN DECLINE

Democracy in Decline

Steps in the Wrong Direction

JAMES ALLAN

McGill-Queen's University Press
Montreal & Kingston • London • Ithaca

© McGill-Queen's University Press 2014

ISBN 978-0-7735-4350-8 (cloth)
ISBN 978-0-7735-9192-9 (ePDF)
ISBN 978-0-7735-9193-6 (ePUB)

Legal deposit second quarter 2014
Bibliothèque nationale du Québec

Printed in Canada on acid-free paper that is 100% ancient forest free (100% post-consumer recycled), processed chlorine free

McGill-Queen's University Press acknowledges the support of the Canada Council for the Arts for our publishing program. We also acknowledge the financial support of the Government of Canada through the Canada Book Fund for our publishing activities.

Library and Archives Canada Cataloguing in Publication

Allan, James, 1960–, author
 Democracy in decline: steps in the wrong direction / James Allan.

 Includes bibliographical references and index.
 Issued in print and electronic formats.
 ISBN 978-0-7735-4350-8 (bound). – ISBN 978-0-7735-9192-9 (ePDF). – ISBN 978-0-7735-9193-6 (ePUB)

 1. Democracy. I. Title.

JC423.A58 2014	321.8	C2014-900650-0
		C2014-900651-9

This book was typeset by Interscript in 10,5/13 Sabon.

Contents

Preface   vii

Introduction   3

PART ONE COUNTRIES IN DECLINE   6
 United States   9
 New Zealand   20
 Canada   25
 United Kingdom   30
 Australia   34

PART TWO CAUSES OF DECLINE   41
 Judges   42
 International Law   83
 Supranational Organizations   107
 Undemocratic Elites   121

PART THREE COMPLICATIONS MASKING DECLINE   128

PART FOUR CHALLENGES THREATENING MORE DECLINE   144

Concluding Remarks   160

Suggested Further Reading   167

Notes   169

Index   179

Preface

This book is part lament and part call to arms. It's a book about the decline of democracy. The focus, though, is not global or worldwide, pointing out slippage in this newly democratic Third World country, or problems in a Latin American one, or even faults in a Western European country such as Italy. No, the focus of this book is exclusively on five of the oldest democracies in the world, countries that before just about anywhere else worked out how to count everyone as equal and then let the numbers count as a way to resolve debatable and contested social policy line-drawing disputes.

I refer to the Anglo-American democracies of the United States, the United Kingdom, Canada, Australia, and New Zealand. These are among the handful of the world's long-established, most stable democracies and two of them are among the most important countries on earth. The United States is the world's only superpower at present.

And I will argue in this book that democracy is in decline in all five of them. It is in decline, too, in most of the rest of the rich, developed world though my overwhelming focus will be on America and the anglosphere.

In a world where the number of democracies has increased considerably in the last few decades, from 40 or so in the mid-1970s (with but a handful outside the West), to some 75 by 1990 (which by then was about half the world's independent states), to roughly 115 democratic countries in 1995, to nearly 120 in 2005, my claim about democratic decline may initially strike many as a tad implausible. But having dozens of countries move from dictatorship and one-party rule to a set-up that manages to qualify them as plausibly or sufficiently democratic does not in any way prevent backsliding in established democracies over that same period of time. Top-end decline can happen concurrently with bottom end improvements, as many a dieter will confirm.

There are at least five main ways to respond to my lament, or call to action, about the declining fortunes of democracy in the Anglo-American world. Some will say that I am simply wrong on the facts. They will argue that democratic decision-making is not being eroded by unelected judges adopting ever more expansive approaches to interpreting bills of rights, by international law and supranational bodies such as the United Nations and European Union, by the interaction of political correctness and intolerant world views, or by anything else.

That is what they will argue. Yet by the end of this book you will see that they are wrong. The facts are on the side of those of us who see democratic decision-making being eroded.

A variant on this first response is possible too. Here you say the Anglo-American world was never all that democratic to begin with, pointing to the US Senate or the UK's voting system, and so claiming that talk of decline is misleading. I will argue that is wrong too.

Another response, and a surprisingly common one at that, is simply to define away the problem. Here we have the battle over a name: What does it mean to call a decision-making process democratic? It is nowhere near as clear as you might suppose. I think of democracy as being focused on process, on *how* decisions are made. Think of it as a commitment to letting the numbers count and prevail, to majority rules. On my understanding, democracy does not guarantee outcomes that are always good or with which any particular person will always agree. Indeed, in countries of 320 million or 65 million or 35 million people none of us could ever be so naive as to think the majority decision would always align with our own personal values, judgments and preferences.

Think of mine then as a thin or unvarnished or procedural understanding of democracy, one I will expand upon in Part III of this book. On this understanding democracy is but one desirable goal among many. Put differently, democracies can on occasion decide to do things that many people may see as bad things, perhaps to do with not sufficiently protecting liberties or not increasing or redistributing wealth enough. Of course one might, like me, also suspect that majoritarian decision-making, letting the numbers count, gets things right far more often than not – in fact, far more often than other alternatives. Do you think the track record would be better where the final say were left with small elite groups from academia, or from the legal profession, or from those who happen to be well versed in scripture or great philosophy texts or military manuals or the writings of John Maynard Keynes? I certainly don't.

Leaving that battle till later, however, my point here is that when you think of democracy as a procedure for making decisions in a world where smart, nice, well-informed people will and do regularly disagree, democracy does not guarantee good outcomes. Yes, you might on average think those outcomes have a better likely batting average, or hit rate, than any other way of making decisions. Indeed that is precisely what I happen to think. But that assertion about what plays out best in the world of politics does not change the fact that democracy on this procedural, majoritarian, letting-the-numbers-count understanding just describes a way of making decisions. It is not a guarantee of the goodness or rightness or superior moral credentials of those decisions in any or all instances.

Issues can and do arise, in other words, where the majority speaks and you think it has spoken foolishly or wrongly or in a panic.

The second way to reject this book's argument about the decline of democracy in the United States, Britain, Canada, Australia, and New Zealand, then, is simply to think of democracy in much fatter, more morally pregnant terms. "When I use a word," said Humpty Dumpty, "it means just what I want it to mean." Likewise, many people[1] just use the term *democracy* to mean a great deal more than the process of majoritarian decision-making. For them, being a democracy and describing some country's system as "democratic" carries with it an additional assertion that the decisions taken have reached a certain level of goodness or acceptability or rights-respectingness. In other words, for them, the noun *democracy* and the adjective *democratic* do not simply refer to *how* decisions are made, they also (to some extent or other) refer to the quality of those decisions.

So a country that, let us imagine, tramples on individual rights or adopts regulations that severely disadvantage a particular religion or nationalizes all property, does not get to be called a democracy. Democracies, on this understanding, only include places where the decisions made are considered good ones, or at least not terribly bad or wicked ones.

People who use the word *democracy* in this fat, morally pregnant way want it to tell you two things, one about how a decision was made and another about the goodness or appropriateness of that decision. Democracy, on this view or understanding, means both a statement that decision-making is being done by some majoritarian process as well as a claim that the decisions pass some pre-established moral threshold.

This fat, substantive, morally laden understanding of democracy is not, in my view, a desirable one. If decisions are made on a fair, open, majoritarian basis then it is better to be able to say "country X is a democracy, but one that now ignores many individual rights and tramples on various economic freedoms" than to say it is not a democracy. We need to keep separate the issue of how a country makes its key decisions, on the one hand, and on the other whether some or all of us think those decisions are generally or overwhelmingly rights-respecting or freedom-protecting or morally palatable.

Put bluntly, there are good grounds for leaving yourself room to be able to say "that country is a democracy, but it is doing very wrong-headed, even wicked, things." And that is true despite you, and I, also thinking that most of the time, overwhelmingly perhaps, democracies do not do wicked things or even that no other decision-making procedure would, on the whole, make better decisions.

Whether you agree with that, or not, notice how the adoption of a fat, morally pregnant understanding of democracy makes it so hard for anyone to claim – as I am going to do in this book – that democracy is in decline. If I point to the European Union, say, and show that decisions are being made by a coterie of unelected bureaucrats the response can always be "well, perhaps, but only when the decision is the right one to further integration or reduce carbon emissions or strengthen monetary union."

If decision-making is taken out of the hands of the majority in order to get what is thought by some, or even many, to be the right or proper outcome, and the very idea of democracy includes some component of getting decisions right, or achieving good outcomes, then any complaint about a decline in democracy can be turned into an argument about whether the decisions made by some group other than the majority were, or were not, in fact the right or best or appropriate ones.

You end up arguing about *what* was decided (namely about outcomes), not about *how* decisions were made (namely about process).

And that makes it much more difficult to argue that ever more important decisions in the Anglo-American world are not being made on a democratic basis, such as when Californian and later the very top national judges overrule the state legislature (and indeed the people voting in a referendum) on same-sex marriage or the US Supreme Court overrules Congress about the 2002 McCain–Feingold Act limits on campaign financing. If we are forced to include an element of whether this or that course of action was right or wrong in our claims about what was the democratic option, then any book like this one about democracy is forced into arguing for or against – defending or attacking – a series of moral positions about same-sex marriage, abortion, international criminal jurisdiction, how best to finance elections, you name it. This makes it much harder, indeed much more prone to reasonable disagreement between smart, nice, well-informed people, to make claims about democratic decline.

So I will foreclose any such attempt to define away the problem. When this book argues that democracy and democratic decision-making are under threat, in decline, and in need of bolstering, it will refer to democracy in the thin, unvarnished sense of majoritarianism and counting all citizens as equals and letting the numbers count. There will be no defining away of the problem. And people inclined to adopt a more morally laden understanding of democracy should have no difficulties in putting that aside temporarily for the purposes too this book.

There are three more main ways to respond to this book's argument that democracy is in decline in the United States, in Britain, in Canada, in Australia, and in New Zealand. Two of these gambits are related. One is to hold yourself out as agnostic about the virtues of democratic decision-making, in the thin, procedural sense just sketched above. If you are uncertain about the merits of democracy then whether or not it is in decline probably won't worry you too much.

Connected to that, but taking an even harder line, is to say some things matter to you more than democracy. Of course if that be true, then a decline in democratic decision-making need not be at all worrying. Whether it is or is not a concern will depend on the reasons why the voice of the majority has been trumped.

Go back to my earlier mention of same-sex marriage in California and recall the basic history. Pro-same-sex marriage advocates, unable to convince the Californian legislature, opted to go through the courts and in May 2008 the California Supreme Court ruled 4–3 in their favour. The judges struck down a statute of the elected legislature confining valid marriages to those between a man and a woman.

This happened in the case known as *In Re Marriage Cases*.[2] The decision was both highly criticized and highly praised, largely depending on the writer's attitude toward the outcome. However, California being one of the US states (along with Oregon and a few others) where there is an especially big dollop of direct democracy, opponents of the court's ruling were not finished. They gathered enough signatures to have a ballot proposition put to a citizens' initiated referendum that would change the California Constitution, adding a section that would read, "Only marriage between a man and a woman is valid or recognized in California." This was the wording of the earlier statute the judges had overturned.

This ballot initiative was known as Proposition 8. Those in favour of it spent $40 million in the campaign leading up to the referendum, and those opposed spent even more, some $43 million. This was one of the largest amounts spent on a campaign ever, excluding presidential campaigns.

When the day of the referendum came, voter turnout was just a shade under 80 per cent. Proposition 8, which would restrict marriage to heterosexual couples, was approved by just over 52 per cent of voters. That meant the State Constitution had been changed.

Winning the referendum and having Proposition 8 approved by a majority of the voters did not, however, end matters. The losers went straight back to the courts, this time to have Proposition 8 itself overturned. When this didn't happen in the Californian State courts, and the proposition was upheld as consistent with the State Constitution but not backdated,[3] the federal courts were the obvious next port of call.

Eventually the issue reached the country's top judges in the case of *Hollingsworth v. Perry* and in June 2013 the US Supreme Court decided the case, 5–4, in favour of same-sex marriage proponents on procedural grounds (namely that if the California government would not defend the ban on same-sex marriage then proponents of Proposition 8 could not do so either; they lacked standing – meaning that the majority of Californians who voted for Proposition 8 had their views trumped by the judges, however indirectly).

And because many, many people celebrated that judicial outcome, I recount the outlines of this struggle here simply as an example that for many people some things matter more than democratic input and majoritarian decision-making. For many proponents of same-sex marriage in California, and elsewhere, what matters is getting it legalized. If that requires the unelected judges to do so by adopting some sort of "living-constitution" interpretive technique or to condone an elected government not defending in court the laws on its statute book, and if that means overruling the views, values, opinions, judgments or preferences of the majority of Californians, so be it. Majoritarian decision-making be damned!

For those people, the perceived rightness or justice of their cause matters more than democracy. The fact there is reasonable disagreement among smart, well-informed, nice, reasonable people on the issue does not lead them to want this issue decided by a letting-the-numbers-count process. Quite the contrary, they want their view of what is morally just and right to be upheld and implemented despite theirs being a minority view (at least outside the ranks of the judiciary), or at least they cannot be bothered to wait until they can convince enough others that theirs is no longer the minority view. In shorthand terms we can think of this attitude as one favouring right outcomes, or rather the particular person's judgment about right outcomes, over best or more defensible processes. What is the most legitimate way to make decisions in a large group where people disagree takes second place for these people to getting what they judge to be the politically or morally right thing adopted.

Contrast that California history with the State of New York's, where the elected legislature, not the judges, legislated for same-sex marriage. The difference in terms of legitimacy is stark.[4]

Now that brief account glosses over certain complexities such as the relationship between representative democracy and direct democracy as well as finessing when it is that we can be satisfied that a vote really is measuring and determining the views of the majority. And that leads on to the fifth possible way to respond to this book's argument about the decline of democracy. People here attack the majoritarian credentials of elected legislatures, often by pointing to perceived flaws in the voting system being used to choose its members. From there, say from the claim that some particular elected legislature is itself deficient in majoritarian terms, they then move on to embrace a powerful role for unelected judges on the basis that the legislature itself is not perfect as regards democracy.

But this fifth way to respond to my lament about the decline of democracy misses the obvious rejoinder that for any elected legislature in the United States, the UK, Canada, Australia, and New Zealand – whatever the flaws you might perceive in the voting system used to choose its members and however far short you may think it falls from embracing some ideal of the popular will or Rousseau's General Will – that elected legislature will nevertheless have massively more majoritarian and "letting-the-numbers-count" credentials than will nine unelected top judges. So in any head-to-head comparison it is clear and beyond argument where the democratic legitimacy chips lie. And so this fifth way to respond to my lament amounts to a misdirection argument; it is a very weak argument. What matters is how proposals fare in comparative terms, not how they fare held up against some perfect ideal.

In a book such as this, not all of the complexities thrown up by these five possible ways to respond to my claim that democracy is in decline can be fully explored, though we will return to consider them in more depth below. Of course for those for whom achieving or fulfilling some other value or outcome matters more than how that is done, then any lament about a decline in democracy is likely to fall on deaf ears. Yes, sure, if the majority view is trumped as regards an issue where they happen to agree with the majority, then of course they will be as much a partisan of democracy as the next man or woman. But when they disagree with the majority, and the trumping by some elite minority favours a value they hold dear, that is when their attachment to democracy will be tested; that is when the temptation is greatest; that is when a lament about democracy being in decline is easiest to ignore; that is when we need to rack the value and find the virtue of democracy.

In this book I will argue that none of those five potential responses to my claims about democratic decline is attractive or stands up to probing and experience. Democracy in America and the anglosphere is in decline, and that is a bad thing. It is a very bad thing indeed.

Think of the remainder of this book then either as a call to action, if you are optimistically inclined, or as a lament, if you are more pessimistic or fatalistic.

I suppose the fact I have written this book decrying the decline of democracy in our five countries suggests that I myself am on the optimistic end of the scale, that I think we can reverse these declines, though we need first to be aware they are happening.

Certainly I am very much a partisan of democracy. I hope to make you one too.

And that leaves only my desire to thank my wonderful family who made it easier than it should have been to write this book, my beautiful wife Heather and my two great kids Cameron and Bronwyn. And thanks too go to my law school at the University of Queensland in Australia which has always treated me very well, and to the magnificent University of San Diego law school where I finished up this book while on sabbatical the first half of 2013.

The comparatively short section in this book on international law's reach and effects on democracy was written first for this book, but then adapted for a law review article in the *San Diego Law Review*. At the time of writing it is not clear which will appear first.

DEMOCRACY IN DECLINE

Introduction

Let me say it again. Democracy is in decline in the Anglo-American world consisting of the United States, United Kingdom, Canada, Australia, and New Zealand. The trend is bad and it needs to be reversed. We need to stop judges adopting ever more expansive and externally unconstrained approaches to interpreting key legal documents. We need to cabin the use of foreign and international law as guides to giving meaning to domestic law by those same judges. We need legislatures to think again about inserting potentially sweeping reading-down interpretive mandates (or "do everything you judges possibly can to read all other statutes in a way that you, the judges, think is rights-respecting") into statutory bills of rights. We need to buttress national sovereignty against the inroads and over-reach of supranational institutions and international law. We need to rethink the treaty-making process, at least outside the United States.

We need, as well, to recognize that on so many moral issues in society, even when presented in the language of rights, it is simply a fact that smart, well-informed, reasonable people – people with whom you would be happy to share a beer or meal – will and do disagree. They differ on abortion, on same-sex marriage, on the proper balance to be struck between extending criminal procedural entitlements and seeking effectively to catch criminals, and likewise terrorists, just as they differ on the limits to put on speech, the place of religion in public life, and so much more. And when there is this deep-seated disagreement, people on all sides believe theirs is the correct and right and just view. It beggars belief to think otherwise, that I hold my moral views sincerely but those who disagree with me are generally insincere, or wicked, or in need of re-education. The odds of any of us having a direct pipeline to God, as it were, on all these issues and more are laughably and vanishingly small. And anyway, seeking to resolve these fundamental value disagreements by appealing to what is right gets us nowhere. Both sides believe they are right. That path leads you down into a vicious circle. What you need is a dispute-resolving procedure, and counting each of us as equal and letting the numbers prevail – though certainly no guarantee that the right and just outcome will be chosen – is the best and most legitimate method or procedure going in this unavoidable circumstance of living in society with 320 million (or 65 million or 30 million) fellow citizens.

Or rather, this sort of letting-the-numbers-count majoritarian democracy approach to resolving such crucial social disagreements is the least-bad option available. To quote Winston Churchill, "It has been said that democracy is the worst form of government except all those other forms that have been tried from time to time."[1]

Unfortunately, faith in this least-bad choice of democracy has been in decline these past few decades in all the countries we will be considering. Your say on the questions of capital punishment, who can marry, who can enter the country, and plenty more, has gone down in relative terms. The say of certain well-placed elites has gone up.

Of course there is still plenty of democratic decision-making in the anglosphere. It would be foolish to say anything else. These countries are not just the longest-established democracies in the world, their democratic credentials remain the envy of that world, barring perhaps the odd Switzerland here or there. I do not dispute that. I simply say there is less than there was two or three decades ago. I say inroads have been made into that democratic decision-making. I say the trend is pointing the wrong way.

The rest of this book is my attempt to convince you of those claims. First, we will have a closer look at these five Anglo-American countries, starting with the United States which is not just an overall force for good in today's world, it is easily the most important of the countries we will look at and the one most crucial to the long-term fate of a vigorous form of democracy. I call this first part of the book "Countries in Decline."

The book's second part I call "Causes of Decline." This will be the longest part and will contain the bulk of my substantive case, of why I think democracy is in decline.

In the third part of this book I will turn to what I call "Complications Masking Decline." This is where I will respond to a whole host of arguments that serve to deny this decline or to mask it. This third part of the book picks up some of the themes in the preface, and adds to them.

The last part of this book will be noticeably shorter, and more tangential to my case. Part four I have called "Challenges Threatening More Decline."

I will then have some concluding remarks to make on behalf of democracy.

My hope, as I have said, is to convince you in this book that democracy is in decline in America and the anglosphere, that this is a bad thing, and that it needs to be reversed.

PART ONE

Countries in Decline

Anyone who looks at the constitutional arrangements of the United States, Britain, Canada, Australia, and New Zealand will see similarities, copying, a few noticeable innovations, more copying – in short, lots and lots of similarities and sameness, with a bit of difference and the odd bit of marked divergence. This may not surprise many readers as far as Britain and its former Dominions of Canada, Australia, and New Zealand are concerned, though it may surprise some to learn that Australia's founding fathers explicitly copied much from the American model. The Australians copied the American-style genuine house of review Senate, an elected legislative upper house with real power and real democratic legitimacy, something that is not true in Britain, Canada, or New Zealand. The Australians also copied the American desire to have a strong version of federalism,[1] together with the approach chosen to achieve that goal of reserving to the states the powers not granted to the national legislature. Canada, meanwhile, aimed for a much more enervated version of federalism where the powers of the provinces would be specifically enumerated, and thus more limited. At least that was the assumption. The fact that events did not play out as anticipated – that Australia's federalism proved to be insipid and moribund, that America's ended up far less potent and vigorous than envisioned, and that Canada ended up with the strongest powers in the hands of its non-central provincial legislatures – is highly ironic, but does not alter Australia's initial goal of copying the US set-up or even, for that matter, the judge-driven undermining of that goal of having strong states that has taken place since in both Australia and the United States. Even the American model's choice to leave it to each state to appoint its own top judges was copied by Australia, despite Canada having rejected that choice and handed the power to appoint all the top judges for Ontario, Quebec, Alberta, and all the provinces to the federal government.

Less surprising than this Australian emulation of many things American is, say, the great similarity of New Zealand's unwritten constitutional arrangements with those of the United Kingdom, at least in the latter's pre–European Union incarnation. Indeed, today New Zealand is the unwritten constitution jurisdiction par excellence. Its only competitors for that title in the democratic world are that same United Kingdom, now hedged all about by the European Union and the limits on sovereignty it imposes with its written Lisbon Treaty (or written constitution if you say it *sotto voce*) and arguably Israel. Think of New Zealand as the modern-day successor to Britain's World War II constitutional arrangements, and you will not go too far wrong.

There is plenty of other copying among our five countries. Here's one. Canada copied Britain's unelected upper house, misleadingly calling it a Senate and packing it with appointed placemen and political party hacks to the point it has even less legitimacy today than the UK's House of Lords legislative body it set out to copy. At least in the UK the once largely hereditary and now largely appointed but still wholly unelected members of the House of Lords are not paid more than their expenses. In Canada the democratically illegitimate members of the Senate are on full salaries, the equivalent ones to their elected colleagues in the elected lower house of the legislature!

Here's another copied trait. It is the voting system. Few countries outside the English-speaking ones I am focused upon use a first-past-the-post (FPP), winner-takes-all voting system that usually generates strong majority governments with only two main, viable political parties. The United Kingdom uses it. The United States does too, having copied it from the former imperial ruler. Canada uses it too. New Zealand had FPP until 1996 when it switched to a German-style proportional representation (PR) voting system, but the experience there has been mixed and opposition to the new German system remains despite a second successful referendum in late 2011 that supported this new voting system. Meanwhile Australia used FPP until the 1920s when it switched to a preferential voting system, one much, much closer to FPP than to any PR system, and in my view the best voting system in the world, just a bit better than FPP. (And it's a watered down version of that Australian voting system, now labelled as "AV" – alternative vote – that was offered in a referendum to UK voters in 2011 as an alternative to FPP and that was decisively rejected.)

Perhaps the most obvious constitutional characteristic that has been copied is the adoption of a bill of rights. Now these instruments will be at the heart of much of my complaints against over-powerful judges in this book. That said, it is worth being clear how much things have changed in the course of half a century, in the lifetimes of many people still living.

At the end of World War II, not even seven decades ago, there were only two democracies – indeed only two countries – in the entire world with a bill of rights in place. And of those two, France and the United States,[2] only America's was justiciable and could be used by judges to strike down or invalidate statutes or laws enacted by the elected legislature. Some six and a half decades on since the Second World War and every democracy in the world, save for Australia, has one of these instruments, in some form or another, in place at the national level. Of course not all bills of rights are as potent as the American one; not all of them do as much to take what otherwise would be political disputes such as over who can marry, when speech is permissible, whether foetuses can be aborted and by translating them into the language of rights turn them into quasi-legal disputes to be decided by unelected judges rather than elected legislators.

The point, however, is that everyone, or nearly everyone, has one of these bills of rights today. Virtually all democracies have to some extent taken up and copied this American constitutional model. We will see later just how far Britain, Canada, and New Zealand have done so. For now, suffice it to say that the post–World War II era can, in this sense, be seen as the triumph of American constitutionalism. What was an innovation in the late eighteenth century, one built largely on natural law foundations tied to claims about the inherent rights of man, was ignored for a century and a half outside the United States and France. (And who can be sure about France?) Then, rather suddenly, it was copied, tweaked, copied, modified, copied until eventually it was commonplace. Except in Australia.

The rest of this first part of the book will concentrate on setting out a rough baseline for each of our five countries. In order for me to claim democratic decision-making is in decline in the recent past, there needs to be some set-up or arrangement that was previously more democratic, something against which to measure that decline.

That standard or baseline will differ for each of our five countries. Despite all the sketched out similarities and copying noted above, differences clearly exist between each of our countries when it comes to the amount of letting-the-numbers-count decision-making. Before I move to the causes for the decline in such majoritarian resolving of contested social, political, and moral issues, it is worth having a general idea of how each of our five countries is set-up and what scope and role each gives to democracy.

My claim in this book, after all, is certainly *not* that all of these countries put pre-eminent weight on democracy in order to resolve all debatable and contested social issues. Nor is it that each of the five puts an equal amount of weight or trust in democratic means as the others do. My claim about democracy being in decline is a relative one. Each of our five is less inclined or less able to use democratic means than it was not too long ago. So all five, America, Britain, Canada, Australia, and New Zealand, are less democratic than they once were.

Of course the trend is worse in some than others. To be blunt it is worst in the United Kingdom. And this trend is least apparent in Australia. Yet all five suffer from it.

Before moving to part two of this book, and the causes for that decline, let me give you a rough-and-ready sketch of the place of democratic decision-making in each of our five countries, starting with the world's most powerful country – and given its comparative power and military and economic might a remarkably benign one – the United States of America.

UNITED STATES

In many ways the United States is the most democratic system on earth. There are elections for a whole swathe of officials from sheriffs, to school trustees, to district attorneys (the top law official for the city or county when it comes to prosecutions), to electoral returning officers, to coroners, to judges. In fact, in a good many of the fifty states the highest judges for that state are elected. No other country on earth has the same breadth of elected officials and the same reliance on letting the numbers count when it comes directly to choosing the people who will fill these jobs and make these decisions.

On top of that, federalism in the United States works to ensure that decisions about, say, the school curriculum are made at a more local level – so that what students learn differs not just between Massachusetts and Mississippi but sometimes between two or more counties or parts of the same state – than in other democracies, thereby giving more input to more people than in one-size-fits-all, more centralized systems.

Then there is the well-known mobility of Americans, their willingness to move between cities and states in search of jobs and better lifestyles. In some part, at least, this willingness forces decision-makers who set local property tax rates or state income tax levels or who choose whether to build a big stadium to be more responsive.

Take state income tax levels. In Australia, where federalism is moribund, the states have lost this power to the Commonwealth (or federal) government and one-size-fits-all outcomes prevail. In all six states there the exact same level of income tax rates prevail. In America, by contrast, each state decides for itself. Federalism here is competitive, the idea being that out of the mass of competition between the fifty states those over-taxing states will sooner or later be forced to cut taxes and those under-taxing ones to raise them. The former will take too much to keep taxpayers and employers. The latter will provide too few services to keep them. At least as importantly, different tax rates will attract different sorts of people and employers. Some desire premium services and will pay for them. Others will not. Diversity, rather than uniformity, will deliver best consequences. That is the theory. Or put the other way around, federalism is based on competition not co-operation; it is that competition that justifies, or more than justifies, the extra layers and numbers of decision-makers doing the same thing and all the seeming duplication. That and catering to or satisfying a wider array of people's preferences – about tax rates, service provision, tolerating legalized prostitution, pornography, and much else besides – are two of the principal foundations and justifications of federalism.

Whether you accept those benefits of federalism, or not, such decentralization undoubtedly does create more demand for elections and letting the numbers count. It is another significant factor on the plus side of the ledger when it comes to weighing America's democratic credentials.

So, too, is the regular use made of direct democracy, or referenda, in states such as California and Oregon. Only Switzerland gives a bigger role to asking voters directly what they think on major issues, without the filter of representative legislators linked to political parties.

There is yet another way in which the United States seems comparatively more democratic. This time it has to do with the difficulty elite opinion in the United States (imagine, perhaps, the Harvard Law School common room or the *New York Times* daily editorial meeting) has in capturing all the viable electoral vehicles and so shutting off voters' choices on certain issues, say, the desirability of ending capital punishment or of allowing same-sex marriage. In a nutshell, it's harder to shut off choice in the United States than in the UK (where opinion shapers can just shrug, blame Europe, and have all the main political parties offer the same thing) or even Canada (where there is more deference to the unelected judiciary, or so I will say, than in the United States). Meanwhile continental Europe is, in my view, worse again on this "taking debatable issues off the table" front.

One reason why it is harder to impose an elite consensus on American voters has to do with its more wide-open campaign finance rules. People with their own money can enter races and win Republican and Democratic nominations on insurgency tickets fighting the party hierarchies. They are permitted to buy television time to put forward their views. They can bring significant resources to bear in support of their views during decision-making campaigns. On top of that, even where publicly funded and private universities manifest quite startling degrees of consensus of opinion,[3] America has more – significantly more – private research institutes or think tanks that can act as a counterweight. And the broadcast media, if not the print media, exhibit a far greater range of opinion than in Britain, Canada, New Zealand, or Australia. These latter four have nothing comparable to Fox News. Their government funded BBC and CBC and ABC and TVNZ networks rarely veer far from the metropolitan elite's standard centre-left opinions of the day, unless it is to dabble momentarily with a farther left view.

For these reasons and more it is harder to impose the elite consensus on people in the United States (when it comes to abortion or capital punishment or same-sex marriage or to oversight by international institutions) than it is anywhere else in the democratic world. Put differently, it is harder there to turn off the microphone telling us what the majority wants and thinks. (In a more limited sense this point is sometimes summed up by saying that it's hard to end the culture wars in the United States, though the point also extends to taxation, health care, economic policy, and foreign policy.)

Having more scope for more input, and a broader range of input, and often decisive input at that, seems more likely than not to accentuate the role of majoritarian or letting-the-numbers-count decision-making in America. It is another counter on the pro-democracy side of the ledger.

Here is one last factor buttressing the democratic credentials of the United States. It is this: Treaties with other countries (bilateral or multilateral) cannot come into force until they have been passed by the elected upper house of the legislature, the Senate (and on a two-thirds approval basis at that). This is not true in the United Kingdom; it is not true in Canada, nor in Australia, nor in New Zealand. In all of these latter four jurisdictions the executive branch of government can ratify treaties without any veto resting in, or any need to win a vote in, one of the elected legislatures.[4]

That means that President Clinton can sign the Kyoto Treaty but that it will not bind the United States until approved by the Senate (whose approval never ended up being given). The same goes for submitting to an International Criminal Court or any sort of cap-and-trade emissions-trading scheme for carbon dioxide between countries. You will need Senate approval.

The point is that entering into any of these treaties, or any other treaties, is considerably more difficult in the United States in the specific sense that the executive branch of government is forced to obtain the approval of elected legislators. The latter can block the former, something that is simply not true in the UK, Canada, Australia, or New Zealand where the executive branch of government, using the prerogative power, can sign, enter into and ratify treaties.

Of course none of that unique treaty-blocking power in the hands of the Senate need necessarily add to America's democratic credentials. It depends on whether judges these days tend to interpret important domestic legal texts in the light of these signed treaties; it depends too on whether treaties, at least some treaties, tend to be rather vague, amorphous documents deliberately pitched in abstractions that will allow the world's Sudans, Libyas, and Chinas to sign up, insouciant in a way Western democracies are not about how these vague, amorphous treaties will later be given more specific content by international bureaucrats unaccountable to any voters of any nation-state; it depends again on whether international institutions and the bodies run under these treaties tend to be staffed by people whose views and policy preferences are noticeably out of sync with those of the majority of a nation's voters.

If all of those three tendencies and more are true, as a matter of empirical fact – and I will say they all are true – then the American approach to treaties is the more democratic one, the one that does most to let the numbers count and majority opinion prevail.

For all of these reasons there is a very plausible and persuasive case for saying America's is the most democratic system on earth.

There is, however, another side to the story. In other ways the United States is less democratic than Australia and New Zealand, for sure, and arguably than Britain and Canada even. That is because the governmental institutions of the United States were deliberately set-up on a checks-and-balances basis, not least to balance and check the powers of the majority of voters.

Start with the Senate. Yes, this upper legislative house has its members chosen by elections (unlike in Canada or the UK). Yet where elections to the House of Representatives in Congress are based on the roughly equal vote worth of each voter, on dividing the country into more or less equally filled districts, that is plainly not true of the Senate which is composed of two Senators from each state. The votes of Californians and Texans, in other words, count for a huge amount less than those of North Dakotans and Wyoming voters when it comes to picking the Senate. That is because Wyoming's 500,000 people get the same two Senators as California's 37 million people.

So this offends any letting-the-numbers-count principle.

Then there is the filibuster. This is a parliamentary tactic of blocking the passage of legislation by talking the bill out. Senate rules allow forty of the one hundred Senators to do this, to block closure of debate.[5] This compounds the already less-than-majoritarian aspects of the Senate, though attempts to count the twenty lowest population states to arrive at some hypothetical percentage of overall American voters that could block legislation[6] overstate the anti-majoritarian aspects of the filibuster. Such attempts ignore the fact of party politics and that voters in highly populated states do not all vote for one party's candidates and sparsely populated states' the other's. In real life the forty filibustering Senators will come from far more than twenty states, many of which will also have elected a Senator who opposed the filibuster.

Nevertheless, this filibuster tactic clearly accentuates the already countermajoritarian nature of the Senate.

In addition to the Senate another institutional device that tempers majoritarianism in the United States is the Electoral College. Presidents are not elected directly but indirectly. You can receive more overall votes than the other main candidate, and still lose the election, as has happened three times in US history.[7] This is because the United States does not operate a French-style system where the winner of the popular vote wins. Instead, the Electoral College operates as a filter or intermediary, with each of the fifty states sending it a number of delegates in proportion to that state's voting population. Add to that the fact that forty-eight of fifty states award their delegates on a winner-takes-all basis – so that a 51 to 49 per cent win in Florida gets you all of Florida's Electoral College votes or delegates – and you can see that a few close wins in big states such as California, New York, and Texas can deliver more than enough Electoral College votes to outweigh losing lots of other small states by a biggish margin, and on occasion can even make the loser of the popular vote the winner of the election.

Let me be blunt. Choosing who becomes president of the United States is not a purely majoritarian decision-making process. On rare occasions the preponderance of the numbers do not prevail. This is true even though the Electoral College system itself throws up unknowable counterfactuals and undoubtedly affects voting behaviour. So we cannot know for sure how many would-be Republican voters in staunchly Democrat states such as California (or would-be Democrat voters in Republican Utah, say) stay at home because they calculate their votes will not matter – people who in a direct French-style vote *would* go to the polls because their vote *would* count the same as everyone else's and popular vote percentages would determine the winner. We can never know this. We cannot even know for certain if any of those three presidents who won the Electoral College tally but lost the popular vote might have won the latter too in a direct, popular vote contest because people who stayed at home would have voted under a French-style system. No one can be sure how many voters the Electoral College system deters, or possibly even encourages.

That said, and however much it is true that the winner of the Electoral College contest is overwhelmingly likely also to win the popular vote, the fact remains that this is not a decision-making procedure that counts everyone equally and then lets the numbers count. Rather, it builds in a weighting for other non-democratic values, those related to federalism and the importance of the states and, in years gone by, to affording a role to backroom powerbrokers. Indeed, the Electoral College is structured – deliberately and explicitly structured – to accentuate the weight of small population states. This comes about because Electoral College numbers allocated to states are based on the number of Senators per state plus the number of members of the House of Representatives for that state. Yet only the latter of these varies with the population of the state. The number of Senators per state is always two for each and every of the fifty states.

So consider this example. Take a state with a very small comparative population that sends only one member of the House to Congress. That state receives three Electoral College votes, the combination of its Senate representation (2) plus its House representation (1). Now take another US state with ten times the population. Since representation in the House varies with population its Electoral College votes will be the sum of its House representation (10) plus its Senate representation (2), making twelve. But notice what has just happened. A state with ten times the population will, in the Electoral College, have only four times (twelve versus three) the representation. The smaller population state is significantly over-represented in the Electoral College.

Related to this issue of voting, the United States stands out from our other four countries because of the extent of gerrymandering there. In forty-seven out of fifty states the elected legislators, rather than comparatively more disinterested non-politicians, draw the district or constituency boundaries. The trick here is somewhat counter-intuitive. It is *not* to lump together as many as possible of *your* side's voters in a single district. No, it is the opposite of that, to lump together as many as possible of the other side's voters in a single district. You do that by manipulating the geographical shape of those boundaries, often in truly bizarre ways, resulting in districts so odd looking and contrived they can even resemble salamanders or worse. (The term *gerrymander* derives from Massachusetts governor Elbridge Gerry [1812] who signed a bill that redrew district boundaries, one of which appeared to be somewhat in the shape of a salamander.)

The core problem with gerrymandering is that legislators on both sides of politics have a common interest in creating lots of safe districts, ones where the outcomes are overwhelmingly a sure thing. The number of "up for grabs" or marginal districts goes way down. That, in turn, makes winning your party's nomination often harder to do than winning the election against the other side. And that drives many elected representatives to the extremes; they need to cater to those who vote in primaries, generally the most committed and ideological voters; they already know that if they garner the party nomination they'll win the district because of its manipulating shape and the way it was crafted. Put slightly differently, gerrymandering can make things much tougher for centrist politicians, and in both main parties.

So a case can certainly be made that the widespread US practice of gerrymandering affects the majoritarian credentials of its democratic system, at least in the sense of polarizing it more than elsewhere.

Two other design aspects of the US Constitution are obviously undemocratic, in the letting-the-numbers-count sense we are using the term. One is the built-in difficulty of amending that constitution. You need two-thirds of both Houses of Congress and then three-quarters of the states to assent to change. It is a high hurdle, as the historical record clearly shows.[8] In procedural terms, much more is needed than in Australia, where amendment is by referendum (triggered by either House federally) and requires just two things – both a majority of voters nationwide and a majority of voters in a majority of states.[9]

The final anti-democratic aspect of American political and institutional life deliberately designed as such is without doubt the most potent, and controversial. This is the Bill of Rights. As I noted in the preface to this book, America's Bill of Rights is an old one. Indeed, with the French Declaration of the Rights of Man, it is one of the world's two oldest national bills of rights,[10] dating back to the late eighteenth century. Almost all the many others we see around the democratic world are post–World War II creations, most of them fewer than two dozen years old.

Any justiciable bill of rights that can be used in court to empower unelected judges to do something they could not otherwise do has the potential to be anti-democratic in nature. By translating or transmogrifying political disputes into the language of rights, and asking judges (1) what the proper scope of such rights ought to be, (2) when they can justifiably be limited, and (3) how they interrelate, these formerly political disputes (resolved by voting and letting the numbers count) are turned into quasi-legal disputes (resolved by judges, though ironically when *they* disagree the ultimate decision-making rule to resolve their judicial disagreements is also voting or letting the numbers count).

Notice that with any case decided by a top court it is possible that four wonderful, morally enriching judgments or opinions chock full of references to John Stuart Mill, the International Convention on Civil and Political Rights and even Aristotle's *Nicomachean Ethics* will lose out to five pedestrian judgments one suspects were largely written by law clerks. How could it be otherwise? The ultimate way to resolve disputes among judges has to be a procedural one; it cannot be a Spike Lee *Do the Right Thing* or substantive "go with the morally best judgment or opinion or view" because judges flat out disagree about what is right or morally best – just as voters do in the population at large. In that sense, only the size of the franchise differs. The belief that one is aiming for what is right is certainly not restricted to judges. Legislators think this. Voters do too. Nor is the need to justify their decision restricted to judges. Legislators have to do this as well, albeit in less formalized ways than a written judgment or opinion.

I am not aiming at this early stage of the book to pre-empt myself and look at the ways interpretation of a bill of rights has the potential to remove external constraints on what judges can do. That will be a part of my task in part II of this book. Here I merely want to show that justiciable bills of rights are, by design, anti-democratic or countermajoritarian, leaving wholly to one side whether that be a good or bad thing and more so still whether differing approaches to interpreting them can increase the relative power and scope for decision-making of the point-of-application interpreting judges. As I said, that's a task for later on.

For now, think about what a bill of rights is. It is a document that deals in moral abstractions. It lists a series of vague, amorphous rights – to free speech, to freedom of religion, to peaceable assembly, to a fair trial, against unreasonable searches, and more – at a level of indeterminacy that finesses disagreement. Almost everyone, after all, is in favour of the right to free speech (and all the others) up in the Olympian heights of moral abstractions. But down in the quagmire of day-to-day line-drawing decision-making, of applying the abstraction to real-life situations, all you see is disagreement, disagreement, and more disagreement between people who are all smart, well-meaning, and nice. They disagree about how best to regulate election campaigns, including which such regulations are compatible with the amorphous ideal of free speech. Likewise they disagree about when limits can be put on speech, since no one thinks all of us can be left entirely free to say anything we want including inciting others to murder or counselling others on how to make the latest biological weapons. Or think about hate speech and defamatory speech. Here too we will see disagreements, as specific lines attempt to be drawn. The same goes for defining what searches are unreasonable and which religious practices allowable.

The point, then, is that bills of rights play out in the quagmire of social policy–making detail where there is never consensus but always disagreement and dissensus. The indeterminacies of the moral abstractions which are the rights in a bill of rights simply finesse that disagreement and dissensus. They get widespread agreement by focusing on abstract entitlements and leaving for later the need to draw specific lines whose positioning is debatable, contestable and contested. These instruments hand over the final say to judges. Theirs is the last word. Not yours, as a voter, and not your elected representatives' as legislators or members of the executive.

A bill of rights, therefore, reduces democratic decision-making. Judges interpreting these instruments gain decision-making power. Elected representatives of the voters have theirs diminished.

Notice something else, something that distinguishes the anti-democratic or countermajoritarian workings of the US Senate from that of the Bill of Rights. The former, and perhaps in a way federalism too, makes it tougher for the majority to impose its will on the minority. It imposes a supermajoritarian requirement on bringing about change. It allows the minority scope to block the majority, up to a point. It does not, though, allow the minority to bring in changes or adopt policies the majority opposes. Remember, legislation has to get through the House of Representatives too before becoming law. So a Senate can be understood as making majoritarian change harder. The minority has room to block the majority, but not – given that bills must also make their way through the House of Representatives – to bring in changes the majority opposes.

A bill of rights, by contrast, can work to allow the judgments of the minority of voters to trump those of the majority. Provided the judges, or rather a majority of the judges on the top court, interpret the Bill of Rights in this way rather than that, the views of the minority can prevail – on campaign finance regulation, on same-sex marriage, on gun control, on the treatment of suspected terrorists, and so on.

A bill of rights can operate not just to slow down and block the majority but to override and trump it. It is not so much a check on letting the numbers count as it is an anti-numbers-counting device that only the top judges can activate, by majority vote among themselves. Structurally, its countermajoritarian potential is more potent.

That brief accounting of democracy's credentials in the United States – the ways in which it is a remarkably democratic country and the ways in which at the same time its institutions have deliberately been created to limit democratic decision-making – gives us a sense of our baseline or measuring point when it comes to making claims about democracy being in decline there. When discussing America we are not starting from a majoritarian, letting-the-numbers-count nirvana or showcase exemplar. Yes, majoritarian input can be found in more places than probably anywhere else. Yes, it is harder (nay, impossible) to take off the table issues and positions supported by a significant chunk of the population. Yes, there are experiments with direct democracy. And yes, international treaties need to win a vote of elected legislators before being ratified. All these are on the credit side of the democratic ledger.

The debit side is strong too, however. America's unelected judges operating the world's oldest justiciable bill of rights are among the world's most powerful; they can and do regularly strike down laws that have been passed by both Houses of Congress and signed by the president. And the written constitution is hard to amend. And the Senate is designed to have the potential to hamper the will of the majority, forcing it to pass over super-majority hurdles. All these and more are on the debit side of the democratic ledger.

My worry, then, is not that majoritarian democracy is somehow imperfect and curtailed in the United States. It has always been curtailed, and in some ways more so there than in our other countries. No, my worry and the claim of this book is that the inroads into majoritarian, letting-the-numbers-count democracy have increased in the past few decades. And that trend is getting worse. And it needs to be stopped.

In the case of the United States that decline in democracy is overwhelmingly being driven by the judges and how they are going about interpreting domestic legal texts, using approaches whose effect is to reduce (sometimes to vanishing point) the external constraints on what they can do and decide.

However, let us leave that and the causes for this decline in democracy until part II of the book. For now, we will continue with our survey of countries and turn next to New Zealand, in some ways the very antithesis of America, constitutionally speaking, and until relatively recently the most majoritarian, letting-the-numbers-count place on earth.

NEW ZEALAND

Why New Zealand next? After having started by giving a baseline account of the place of democracy and majoritarian decision-making in the United States, an economic and military powerhouse of more than 320 million people, why turn next to a relative minnow of a country of 4 million people situated far off in a corner of the South Pacific Seas? Why consider next the weight put on democracy in this isolated island country whose nearest main neighbour, Australia, is 1,500 miles away across the ocean and the UK and United States are half a world away?

It's a good question. My answer is that New Zealand is today's best contrast to the United States; it has taken the role once allocated to Britain before Britain's membership of the European Union – and that organization's continuing inroads into national sovereignty – made that comparison less stark, less interesting and less informative.

Recall that the United States from its inception had built-in safeguards or roadblocks or hindrances (according to your perspective and inclinations) limiting majoritarian democracy. Indeed it had more of these institutional roadblocks than any of our other four countries.

I turn next to New Zealand because it had (and save for one change has) almost none of these US-style institutional constraints on the majority. It is as close to the flip side of the US coin as one could find as regards institutional faith in democratic decision-making.

To start, and as signalled above, New Zealand has no written constitution. There is no single overarching document that constitutes and details and limits who can legislate and for what, or who can interpret and apply those enactments. There is simply the inherited British constitutional structures founded on unwritten conventions and parliamentary sovereignty – the latter of these being the notion that the elected legislature is legally (*not*, be careful to notice, morally or politically but only legally) unlimited in what it can do and the former being the rules that grew up over centuries of British practice, but that are not enforceable in the courts.

Seen through American eyes this reliance on conventions and lack of legal limits on the legislature can be disorienting. That sense is compounded by the fact that New Zealand is not a federal system, it is a unitary one with no state or provincial governments with specified or reserve areas of jurisdiction.[11] That means there is none of the checks on majoritarian decision-making that flow from federalism.

On top of that, New Zealand has only one legislative chamber. There is nothing equivalent to a Senate, no upper house at all. So that check on democratic decision-making is missing too. To enact a legally valid piece of legislation all that is needed is passage of a bill through this one legislative chamber.

Moreover, until 1990 there was not even a statutory bill of rights in place. New Zealand had a one-chamber legislature, democratically elected, that was legally unlimited in what it could do. No bill of rights. No upper house. No federalism. No written constitution. It was the very antithesis of the American set-up.

This was pretty much the post–World War II British model, one that foreswore all of the formal institutional checks on majoritarian decision-making built into the American model. And yet in 1893 New Zealand was the first country in the world to grant women the vote. It legislated to set aside representation in Parliament for native Maoris in the nineteenth century. It was the first country in the world to enact social welfare protections. And it completely overhauled its protectionist, rather mercantilist economy along remarkably free trade, no subsidies-for-domestic-producers lines in the 1980s.[12] All this was done on a straight majoritarian basis by the country's elected legislators.

In institutional terms, therefore, New Zealand places great trust in democracy. There is no Senate, no filibuster, no written constitution, and until 1990 no bill of rights of any sort to limit the room for action of the elected representatives of the voters. The need or desire to win the elections that had to be held within three years was the main limit on the exercise of power, but that was a political and moral constraint rather than a legal or constitutional one.

That said, from 1990 any baseline account of the place of democracy in New Zealand gets considerably more complicated in at least three ways. First off, a statutory bill of rights was enacted that year. I will say more about these non-constitutional bills of rights – and how they transfer decision-making power to the judges, not least by directing them to interpret all other statutes in a new, less constrained, less focused on the intentions of the law-making legislators, New Age way – in part II of this book.

Here, I will simply assert that this statutory bill of rights proved even more potent than some opponents had feared and most supporters had dreamed. Modelled in some aspects on the Canadian Charter of Rights but shunning other central tenets, this New Zealand variant made inroads into letting-the-numbers-count, majoritarian democracy.

Then there was the FPP voting system. After a binding referendum in 1993 in which just under 54 per cent voted in favour of change, the FPP voting system was changed to a highly proportional one more or less copying Germany's. Whether this move from a FPP voting system to a highly proportional one (known as mixed member proportional,[13] or MMP) better lets the numbers count will depend on how you look at things and what you want your voting system to accomplish.

Under a FPP system, or an Australian-style preferential voting system for that matter, you end up with two main parties. One of these will almost always win a majority of spots in the legislature. That means the two main political parties end up being broad-church or big-tent vehicles – a centre-left one and a centre-right one. The former needs to accommodate (in some shifting, dynamic way) the views of trade unionists, environmentalists, big-government social democrats, human rights lawyers, and more. The latter needs to accommodate (again, in a shifting dynamic way) the views of social conservatives, libertarians and less doctrinaire small-government types, high Tories, anti-deficit fiscal conservatives, and more. Coalition forming and internal bargaining takes place largely in advance of elections and the two resulting broad-church parties take their compromise positions to the voters.

With a proportional voting system it is almost impossible for any single party to win a majority in the legislature – and certainly this is true of the MMP system as it has never happened since its adoption in New Zealand and has happened only once since World War II in Germany. That means that much of the coalition building and negotiating and compromising over policy takes place *after* an election has been held and so cannot then be overruled by the voters. Party leaders go into elections with policies and promises they – and everyone else – know may have to be jettisoned and broken in order to be part of the governing coalition.

Now whether proportional voting systems are more majoritarian can be put to one side for our purposes here, though truth be told I dislike them and would argue they inflate the power of political parties (especially smaller ones) at the expense of voters. Just as awfully, these proportional voting systems are generally sold under the banner of "fairness" – the idea being that a party that wins 38 per cent of the vote should get 38 per cent of the spots in the legislature. In a world where unfairness is not only endemic, but largely in the eye of the beholder, few advocates of proportional voting systems go on to point out the "unfairness" of small parties having disproportionate sway and influence or the "unfairness" of party leaders being able simply to put favoured people high on their list and so ensure they can get pretty much anyone they want into the legislature.

That said, what is important to our discussion here is that MMP-type voting systems can make it harder to get things done in the legislature. If you want bracing economic reforms, say, you need the support of smaller, minor parties. In a unicameral legislature, in a non-federal state, this type of voting system can limit the power of the biggest political parties (for good or for ill).

Put differently, it is possible to think of a voting system as an alternative to the American-style system of built-in limits and checks and balances on power. In the absence of a Senate, over-mighty judges, and an indirectly chosen president, you have a voting system that more or less guarantees no political party can ever win a majority in the legislature.

Again, whether that sort of voting system is a good or wise idea is a wholly different question. And for what it's worth this sixteen-year experiment with MMP still divides New Zealanders, though it was reconsidered and again approved in another binding referendum in late 2011.

Let me finish my sketch of New Zealand's democratic baseline by pointing lastly to the expanding reach there of something known as the Treaty of Waitangi. This very short little document consisting of a preamble and three brief articles was signed back in 1840 at the start of British settlement. It was signed on behalf of the then British government, on one side, and leaders of many of the Maori tribes, on the other. This Treaty of Waitangi had little impact on New Zealand's governing institutions and domestic law from its signing on through the next century and a half. Indeed it was never ratified by Parliament nor incorporated into New Zealand law. But from the late 1980s on it has acquired – or had imputed to it – a newfound status that makes inroads into democratic decision-making. Though still not technically part of New Zealand's domestic law, and hence only operative where statutes incorporate a reference to it, the last quarter century has seen an ever expanding status and force given to this treaty. Some legislation makes undefined reference to its "principles," though few people agree what those might be or even if they can sensibly be said to exist. And the judges have simply invented a partnership doctrine – one between the Crown (meaning the New Zealand government) and Maori (meaning no one knows what for sure in a country where no one is 100 per cent Maori, where many who claim that classification have one-eighth or one-sixteenth or less Maori blood, and where near on half of the 12 to 15 per cent of the population who claim to be Maori live in cities and are not part of the tribal structures).

Suffice it to say that the status given to this Treaty of Waitangi in the last quarter century has been inflated massively. Many today sell it as a founding document that can block, trump and override democratic decision-making.

In New Zealand, then, just as in the United States, we will be able to point to more recent developments that suggest a decline in democratic decision-making. When it comes to the Treaty of Waitangi and New Zealand's statutory bill of rights that trend is in large part being driven by the judges, but by no means exclusively by them. As for the MMP voting system, people disagree on whether it undermines, enhances or leaves much the same that country's majoritarian, letting-the-numbers-count decision-making. If it be the former, though, as I happen to think, the fault this time cannot be laid at the feet of the judges.

That leaves three countries to introduce. I turn next to my native Canada.

CANADA

Canada looks a lot more like the United States, at least at first glance. It has a national Parliament with two legislative chambers. It has federalism. It has a very strong bill of rights with judges who are in my view even more powerful, even more inclined to gainsay the elected legislature, than their American counterparts. It has a written constitution that is comparatively hard to amend, harder than in the United States for many matters.

Of course Canada – as with all the countries we are considering, except for the United States – has a Westminster parliamentary system. It is not a presidential system. The prime minister and all members of Cabinet are also elected members of the legislature. Voters do not vote separately for the executive.

Combine the fact that a prime minister in a Westminster system by definition commands the confidence of the lower house of the legislature – he or she leads the party (or coalition of parties) with majority control of the legislature – with the much greater incentives for elected legislators to toe their party's line in the Westminster world due to the ever-present dangled carrot of a Cabinet position down the road, and you find that prime ministers can almost always get the laws they want passed and enacted into law. Save for the relatively rare minority government situation, and this is certainly true in Canada and the United Kingdom. Even in New Zealand, with its highly proportional German-style voting system that produces perpetual coalition governments, this is generally the case. Australia, which copied much of its constitution from America's, is a Westminster exception on this point.

One reason prime ministers in Canada know that they can almost always get their agendas enacted into law is that bicameralism is a sham. The Canadian upper house, also called a Senate there, is not chosen by elections, by letting the numbers count even in a distorted way. It is in no sense a democratic body. Senators are appointed by the government of the day as vacancies arise and can remain until they are age seventy-five. Put bluntly, the Canadian Senate is composed of placemen, party political hacks, and time servers, leavened only slightly by the odd well-known sports figure or success story to give a fig leaf of cover for the others. Lacking any and all democratic credentials, the Senate has no legitimacy. And so it almost never acts. Bills passed by the elected lower house in Canada overwhelmingly get rubber-stamped by the Senate, with a few extremely rare exceptions such as letting a bill just languish in the upper house when it mandates bilingual judges in the top court.

You could say that Canada has bicameralism in name only,[14] something you could say of the UK as well (though at least their members of the upper house are not paid full salaries and pensions as they are in Canada, receiving only per diem expenses in the House of Lords). Meanwhile New Zealand as we have seen does not pretend. It is a unicameral system. Only Australia of our non-American countries has a genuine upper house of review that can, and does, block and veto bills passed by the lower house.

Canada differs from the American set-up in other ways too. Despite being a federal system, it was designed to be highly centralized. One of the ironies of history is that Canada's provinces – whose powers were specifically enumerated on the assumption that doing that would be more limiting than simply reserving to them everything not explicitly given to the centre – have turned out to be more powerful with more scope for decentralized decision-making than US states. (Australia's federalism is so emasculated that its states, which no longer can even set their own income taxes, are not really in the same league for purposes of comparison as Canada's provinces where some even decide for themselves big elements of their immigration policies.)

This unplanned result of today's very strong provinces, however, does not change other highly centralized realities in Canada today. For instance, criminal law is made by the centre in Ottawa for the whole country. And all the top judges are appointed by the federal government in Ottawa. No province can choose its own top judges. So if the political sentiment in one province, say Alberta, is noticeably to the right of the country as a whole, all of Alberta's top judges will nevertheless be appointed by the party in power nationally, in Ottawa. This is true even if a left-of-centre party is in office nationally for most of four decades, from the mid-1960s till the mid-2000s.

In fact, some American commentators look up at Canada and think they are seeing a remarkably apolitical top judiciary compared to their own, where ideological fault lines are clear and obvious. But that is a mistake. What they are actually seeing is ideological consensus, a consensus that flows from the fact one political party has made the vast preponderance of judicial appointments across the entire country, and perhaps too from the fact Canada (and all our other countries) lacks a US-style Senate confirmation process for appointments.

If you want a rough idea of how this plays out in, say, Alberta, imagine that President Obama or President Clinton could simply appoint – with no need for any confirmation process – all the top state judges for Texas and Utah. Eventually they would find a few Democrats to appoint. And after forty years of mostly Democrat administrations in Washington (to keep the analogy with Canada going), the US judiciary nationwide and on the top state courts would look a lot less ideologically fractured – would look considerably more apolitical – than it does under the existing US system for appointing judges. But that would be because the judges who had been appointed were grossly unrepresentative of the range of voters' value preferences.

Canada, then, was designed to be a more centralized federal state than the United States, though provincial powers have confounded that expectation and in various ways – despite criminal law-making being a federal power – surpass those of their neighbouring American states. But as far as the vast array of elected US officials right down to dog catcher goes, Canada is far less democratic. And the media is more monolithic in its outlook. And there is nothing like the broad spectrum of think tanks and research institutes. And treaties get made and ratified solely by the executive under the prerogative power,[15] with no ability for the elected legislature to gainsay or veto them.

On these counts Canada looks noticeably less democratic than its southern neighbour. On the other hand, we have seen already that that check on letting-the-numbers-count majoritarianism (that a two-members-from-each-state elected Senate provides) is absent in Canada. What the majoritarian lower house – the House of Commons

– wants enacted, it gets (except in rare cases of minority government when unelected Senators, all simply appointed and in this scenario perhaps chiefly appointed by the previous government, can allow a few bills to languish until the end of the parliamentary session). That means the letting-the-numbers-count credentials of Canada's national legislature surpass America's, though the sometimes significant differing sizes of Canada's national constituencies or districts – with some in Prince Edward Island and Quebec, say, having considerably fewer voters than others in Ontario, Alberta, and British Columbia – somewhat erodes that superior majoritarian credential.

As for the anti-democratic, or countermajoritarian, effect of a powerful bill of rights, the comparison between Canada and the United States is a wash. It's a toss-up. Both have potent bills of rights empowering powerful judiciaries that regularly gainsay and overrule the elected legislature and strike down its enactments.

Some are tempted to point to section 33 of Canada's Charter of Rights as evidence that Canada's judges under that instrument make fewer inroads into majoritarian decision-making than American judges under their Bill of Rights. Again, this is a mistake. Section 33, sometimes known as an override provision, allows the legislature to declare that an act or statute will operate, notwithstanding some of the enumerated rights in the Charter of Rights.

That temptation to point to section 33, alas, is better off resisted. This section 33 does nothing, in practice, to bolster letting-the-numbers-count decision-making. First off, section 33 applies only to some, not all, of the enumerated rights. Secondly, it allows legislation to be exempted only for five-year periods (though the exemptions can be renewed). Thirdly, it cannot be used retrospectively, only prospectively – or so the top Canadian judges have interpreted the reach of section 33.

But most damningly, this section 33 notwithstanding clause that more than a few commentators and law professors point to as giving Canada's system better democratic credentials than America's is a facade in practice. It has never been invoked, not one single time in the entire three decade plus existence of the Charter of Rights, by the Canadian Parliament.[16]

Given some of the contentious decisions by the Canadian Supreme Court – and all top courts indulging in this sort of activity inevitably have to make some moral and political calls, at least a few of which will be quite unpopular – why has the Canadian legislature never once invoked section 33 and at least temporarily trumped the judges?

I think it is in part, perhaps in large part, because of the wording of section 33. This provision implies, incorrectly and inaccurately, that its purpose is for elected legislators to override the Charter of Rights itself – as opposed to overriding disputed and debatable judicial interpretations of the Charter.

Put differently, Canada's section 33 makes a response by the elected legislature extremely unlikely by making it seem as though legislators, were they to invoke section 33, are against the Charter of Rights and against rights rather than simply that they are contesting some highly debatable interpretation of one or more of the amorphous and indeterminate rights provisions, substituting for five years their own highly debatable interpretation for that of the judges.

Or put differently yet again, this section 33 skews what is really going on. It confirms the judges as the authoritative and unerring arbiters of what our rights are down in the quagmire of social policy line-drawing – even when the judicial vote is 5–4 in some case and on the implicit grounding that judges have some pipeline to God on these highly debatable and contentious issues on which smart, nice, reasonable people simply disagree – and then leaves the legislators with a power to say, in effect, "Okay, but we're going to take your rights away." Framed like that it is an unusable power in all but the most extreme imaginable circumstances.

Worse than that, it mischaracterizes what is usually going on. The legislators (or rather a majority of legislators) do not agree with the top judges (or rather a majority of the top judges) about how best to understand the appropriate reach of and scope of and reasonable limits on rights in some particular case. That is what is going on, not some pervasive desire by legislators to take rights away.

Yet section 33 characterizes the dispute as though the judges' view on rights is unerring and legislators invoke the section to take rights away, not to offer a different or better view on rights and their reach. And with that characterization it may not be overly surprising that section 33 is never used, has become in practice otiose, and in no way justifies any claims to its making Canada's bill of rights less democratically objectionable than America's. Indeed, given that the Canadian judges sometimes point to section 33 to justify their adventurism – by saying, rather disingenuously, "Oh well, the legislature can always override this ruling" – it may even serve the unintended aim of making Canada's top judges even more willing to gainsay the elected branches than America's top judges, whom everyone knows have no fig leafs to hide behind as regards who has the last word.

There is even a Canadian (and to a lesser extent American) analogy to what is happening in New Zealand with the judges down there treating the Treaty of Waitangi as a quasi-constitutional source of law. So in Canada the judges treat, say, the Royal Proclamation of 1763 – which is not even an act of Parliament – and certain Indian Treaties (in some cases signed between British soldiers and various eighteenth-century Indian chiefs) in a broadly similar way.

To sum up the situation in Canada, we can say that their judicially operated Charter of Rights makes at least as many inroads into majoritarianism and letting the numbers count as the Bill of Rights does in the United States. With no elected, powerful, favouring-voters-in-small-provinces upper house, and so a lower house that virtually always gets its way, the Canadian legislature is more majoritarian than its neighbour's to the south, though the differential sizes of the districts or constituencies for this lower house gut some of this advantage. Meanwhile Canadian federalism is strong and healthy, but fewer officials are chosen by elections and treaties can be entered into and ratified without the legislature having any say at all of any sort.

Finally, then, there is the question of what has caused and is causing democratic decline in Canada. As with the United States one can say that this decline is overwhelmingly being driven by judges, especially how these judges are interpreting the Charter of Rights that was made part of the Canadian Constitution just under three decades ago in 1982. It is the living-tree or living-constitution approach to interpreting that Charter, one that has virtually no dissenters among the ranks of Canada's top judges, that I will say can serve almost to eliminate external constraints on what judges can do and decide when we turn to the causes of decline in part II of the book.

UNITED KINGDOM

Were I writing this in the late 1960s I could simply tell the reader that the scope for, and place of, democratic decision-making in the United Kingdom was virtually identical to what it is in New Zealand. Sure, there's an upper house in the UK, but it can only delay legislation, not block it. And anyway, that upper house is not an elected body, and so has little legitimacy. So the situation is not all that different from New Zealand's unicameralism.

Other than that, and the absence of New Zealand–style concerns with the Treaty of Waitangi, the UK and New Zealand look near on identical. No written constitution. No federalism. No genuine upper house of review that can block the passage of bills. No bill of rights. As good as it gets, really, in terms of letting-the-numbers-count majoritarian democracy.

Alas, that is the picture from over four decades ago. The picture today is very different indeed, and on almost all the above counts.

First off, the United Kingdom now has a statutory bill of rights, one I will be discussing in more depth later in this book. It is a very potent bill of rights in terms of its capacity to transfer social policy line-drawing power from the elected legislature to the unelected judges. Indeed, some commentators[17] – and let me be clear that these are people who like this statutory bill of rights and who like the much enhanced judicial role – think it gives the top UK judges virtually as much decision-making power as their American judicial counterparts. After all, what is really the difference between the power top American judges have to strike down and invalidate legislation they happen to think is inconsistent with one or more of the vague, amorphous enumerated rights and the power British judges have, when they think legislation is not rights-respecting, to read words in, read words out, give it a meaning clearly not intended by the enacting legislature (even where there is no ambiguity whatsoever) – in short to rewrite the law and legislate from the bench? If anything, the American position is preferable for being more honest and transparent. And I say that from the perspective of a majoritarian, letting-the-numbers-count adherent, of one who dislikes both these sort of judicial forays or activities.

The recent changes to, or transmogrification of, the top UK court from the well-known brand of a committee of the House of Lords to the far grander named – and now separately and expensively housed – Supreme Court are unlikely to lessen judicial adventurism of the sort now on display when interpreting their statutory bill of rights, and on which I will say more later.

A second change in the last few decades when it comes to sketching the place of democratic decision-making, UK-style, is the recent move to a sort of quasi or pseudo-federalism. Scotland and Wales have their own legislatures, albeit with fairly circumscribed powers. The devolved bodies and powers are the result of a simple act of the UK Parliament, and so in theory could be removed in the same way. But political realities make any such attempt implausible in the extreme. Meantime these modest steps certainly do not lessen letting-the-numbers-count decision-making, though it is an issue complicated by the fact that Scotland and Wales have devolved elected legislatures for areas of jurisdiction that England (and the bulk of Britain's population) does not.

Far more straightforward and clear, in terms of its effect on democratic decision-making, is the UK's entry into the European Union or EU, formerly known as the European Economic Community and before that the European Coal and Steel Community. In terms solely of its effect on democracy, and not just for the UK but a good many other member countries too, the effect has been lousy, awful, terrible, pick your favourite pejorative adjective.

If we restrict our gaze to what is generally thought of as the developed democratic world, the EU has pretty much the worst democratic credentials going.[18] It has an elected legislature, true. But it is a legislature that cannot initiate legislation. That job rests with the European Commission, a body of appointed civil servants. Indeed the EU Parliament manages to make Hong Kong's legislature look good in terms of letting the numbers count, and Hong Kong's legislative council still has a host of rotten boroughs – of reserved spots in the legislature for those chosen only by small, select constituencies of businessmen or trade unionists or lawyers and so on. But at least within these highly circumscribed categories people get to vote for the representatives who will initiate, make and repeal the laws. Not in the EU. The legislature there has only a veto of sorts when it comes to law-making.

That means the democratic credentials of the EU come largely in second-hand form, from those of its constituent governments which are all themselves democracies. Alas, for many that is not self-evidently sufficient. It is one thing to cede a good deal of a country's law-making sovereignty to a larger entity, as the UK has done to the EU. It is another to cede it to such a patently democratically deficient supranational organization.

Nor is it just the legislature and how the laws are made that fail the letting-the-numbers-count smell test. The constituent governments of the EU, admittedly democracies, have also again and again made changes to the structure and workings of the EU without seeking any democratic mandate beyond the approval of the same politicians who run the system. It is clearly and evidently a top-down project driven by the elite. So in that sense even the Council of Ministers, made up of the heads or proxies of the constituent governments and the third arm (along with the appointed Commission and neutered Parliament) of the EU governing machinery, is democratically suspect. It cannot easily, and sometimes ever, be held accountable for the decisions it makes.

When it comes to treaties meant to increase the EU's powers we see that many governments do not offer its citizens a say, and those that do just keeping asking till they get the answer they want.

None of this is to deny that the single market is efficient and wealth creating; or that French and German co-operation is desirable; or that pan European alignment may be a force for good in the world (though I would argue that the Common Agricultural Policy and its farm protectionism undoubtedly is a malign force in today's world). No, there are clearly some good outcomes to be associated with the EU. My point is just that it is not a very democratic supranational body and its ever expanding reach has been brought about in a way that would fail to achieve even bare passing marks on a majoritarian, letting-the-numbers-count scorecard.

The UK's adoption of the most recent power transfers from constituent governments to the EU, namely the Lisbon Treaty, is a perfect case in point. This Lisbon Treaty contains roughly 99 per cent of what had been in the earlier mooted new EU draft Constitution. All the main UK political parties promised (prior to the 2005 election) a referendum on whether to sign up. But after earlier referenda in France and Ireland rejected this draft constitution, its name was changed to the Lisbon Treaty, a few fairly trifling provisions were removed, and it was passed by the UK Labour Party government through Parliament without the promised referendum. Once enacted the Conservative Party and Liberal Democrats withdrew the offer of a referendum saying it was too late.

The result is that even more of the laws that affect Britons are made by the EU. And note that EU law trumps UK law when the two are inconsistent. Or at least that is true up to the point Britain's Parliament passes a law to leave the EU.

In part II of this book, when considering the causes of democratic decline, I will pursue this further. Suffice it here to say that with its entry into the supranational and seemingly non-stop jurisdiction-expanding EU, and with its new judicial power-enhancing statutory bill of rights (known as the Human Rights Act), the UK has seen the biggest decline in majoritarianism over the last few decades of any of the Anglo-American countries we will be looking at. It has dropped the most from its earlier baseline. The trend there is the worst.

Put more bluntly, I would say letting-the-numbers-count majoritarian decision-making is in a worse state there today than in the United States, Canada, New Zealand, or Australia, and perhaps by a fair bit.

AUSTRALIA

If the UK has fared worst, Australia has fared best. Not only is the trend in favour of withstanding inroads into democratic decision-making best there of all our countries, it also looks best in absolute terms. No national bill of rights of any sort. No ceding of law-making power to a democratically deficient – or make that highly deficient – supranational body such as the EU. Top judges who are comparatively restrained in their interpretive approach, where that means a reticence to give terms a scope and reach that has the effect of increasing the judges' own last-word decision-making powers.

I mentioned above that Australia copied much of its written constitution's architecture and key provisions from the United States, most obviously as regards bicameralism and federalism. Yet one thing the founding fathers Down Under considered, debated, but then explicitly rejected back in the late 1800s was a bill of rights. They were happy for there to be Senate-style limits on majoritarianism where minorities could sometimes block majorities, but they opted to forswear the judge-driven bill of rights outcomes where, on occasion, minorities could do more than block majority initiatives and preferences; they could use the bill of rights to impose their policy preferences (once suitably transliterated into the language of vague, amorphous rights whose reach and scope and limits were indeterminate until the top echelon of the judiciary had spoken) on the majority as we see today in various jurisdictions with issues such as abortion, same-sex marriage, capital punishment, aspects of immigration, swathes of criminal procedure, gun control, and more.

Interestingly the push for some sort of bill of rights for Australia has intermittently been revived. Twice, in 1944 and 1988, constitutional amendments were proposed along these lines and defeated soundly. Today the push by proponents is to sidestep the machinery of constitutional amendment and try for a statutory bill of rights along the lines of the UK model. But opposition in Australia is more pronounced and thus far opponents and skeptics – visible in both the main political parties – have kept that at bay too.

One of the reasons Australia's political elite were unable to impose a constitutional bill of rights is that those same founding fathers did not just copy from the United States. They copied as well from Switzerland. They ensured that proposed constitutional amendments had to be put to the people, not just to the state and national politicians in the legislatures around the country.

So to succeed, a proposed constitutional amendment in Australia has to win a national referendum. It must receive over half the votes nationwide (and surely this is as majoritarian a criterion as any imaginable, remembering that voting in Australia is compulsory). As well, in a nod toward federalism, it must also win a majority of votes in a majority of states. This means a proposed amendment could win a majority of votes in Australia as a whole and still be defeated for failing to win in more than half the states. (This most obviously might happen when the smaller states in terms of population are opposed but one or two of the big population states are strongly in favour.)

As events have played out, however, there have been 44 proposed constitutional amendments in Australia and all but 8 have failed. More tellingly still, save for five times, all the failures were because the majority of Australians opposed the mooted amendment, an outcome no letting-the-numbers-count majoritarian could fault on procedural grounds. Fewer than a half dozen times, ever, has the majority said "yes" nationwide but the second limb – the need for a majority of voters in a majority of states – not been met.

This Swiss-style aspect of direct democracy when it comes to amending the Australian constitution ties in with what I mentioned above about the lack of a national bill of rights in Australia. Those proposing one could not convince the people; they twice failed to get a majority of Australians to say "yes," and they failed badly. This is true even though they no doubt could have prevailed had they only had to do what happened in Canada when Canadians got their 1982 Charter of Rights – namely, get the national Parliament and sufficient provincial (or state) legislatures to agree, without any of them (not one) holding an election on the issue.

The absence of any sort of bill of rights to limit Australia's elected national legislature clearly enhances the letting-the-numbers-count, majoritarian credentials there. It also flows over into a noticeable chunk (if still a minority) of top judges' unwillingness to adopt living-constitution- or living-tree-type interpretive approaches that impose far fewer external constraints on what they can do at the point of application with the words of statutes or the constitution. This judicial constraint or reticence also increases the pool of decisions that will be decided on a letting-the-numbers-count, majoritarian basis.

Australia is not perfect, of course, even on the rights front. In the early 1990s the judges on Australia's highest court – not all that long after the most recent failed constitutional amendment attempt to have adopted a rather modest sort of bill of rights – simply invented out of thin air the doctrine of implied rights or more specifically an implied freedom of political communication.[19] So despite the fact the drafters and approvers of Australia's Constitution had considered and explicitly rejected a US-style Bill of Rights, well aware that they were deliberately shunning any sort of First Amendment type judicially enforced guarantees in favour of leaving the resolution of these contentious, debatable line-drawing exercises to the elected legislature, the judges stepped in and said they could imply into the text and structure of the Australian Constitution a similar sort of rights guarantee, albeit an implied rather than explicit one.

Put differently, the Australian High Court disconnected the notion of implication from any intentions of any real life drafters (or approvers) of that constitution. They turned it into a sort of gazing at tea leaves in tea cups exercise or concept that to the disinterested outside observer looks much the same as just making it up on the basis of current judicial preferences. They simply invented out of whole cloth a so-called freedom of political communication.

Now I happen to be a big believer in American-style wide-open free speech with few constraints indeed on what people can or should be able to say. So I like the outcome here. Yet how it was achieved was patently illegitimate and divorced from anything to do with interpretation. It was plain out judicial construction, at least to my way of thinking. And the test of one's commitment to democracy comes not in easy situations when one disagrees with the judges' override of the legislature; it comes when one substantively agrees with the judges but thinks decision-making legitimacy, interpretive honesty and long-term consequences point against them doing what they did.

Anyway, this making-it-up aspect made these judicial decisions controversial. I think it made them considerably more controversial than they would have been had there been a rights-based text anywhere that the judges could have pointed to and used to get the same result. And that limited the judges' preparedness to go very far down this implied rights path, though in the last few years there have been new signs of movement on this front. Nevertheless, compared to what judges in Canada and the United States, and even the UK and New Zealand, have done with their explicit bills of rights, Australian judges have gone very little distance indeed with their made-up implied rights doctrine. Even the freedom of political communication is not anywhere near the same scope as a personal right to free speech. And that's a good thing if you're a majoritarian democrat because it leaves much more to be decided by the elected Parliament. Implied rights, given the lack of legitimacy feel to them, end up limiting what the judges can do. They make massively fewer judicial inroads into democratic decision-making than when there are explicit rights in a bill of rights.

Related to that, it seems worth pointing out here that when it comes to, say, the harshness of anti-terrorism measures or what scope people have to speak their minds (ranging from things that might influence election campaigns through to things that some groups might consider to be hate speech) or the ability to practise one's religion or assemble or associate and so on, Australia without a bill of rights looks at least as rights-respecting a place to live as the UK, United States, Canada, or New Zealand. At any rate I think that is plainly the case unless one assumes rights issues, and how best to resolve them, are *not* highly debatable and are best decided by committees of ex-lawyers with extra special moral perspicacity.

My point is that Australia scores highest of all our countries on this democratic front because it still, rather luckily and remarkably, lacks a national bill of rights. Indeed the way these instruments are today being interpreted – as changeable, living documents whose meaning judges can alter through time – will be one of the main focuses of part II of this book. Suffice it here to note that the ever expanding reach of these present-day interpretive approaches that forswear locked-in meanings takes off the table a fairly attractive middle-road or halfway option. This is the path whereby rights guarantees are interpreted to provide an unchanging floor-level protection above which other issues such as abortion or same-sex marriage are to be resolved by letting-the-numbers-count democracy. But I leave consideration of that for part II of this book.

Let me finish this sketch of the place of democratic decision-making in Australia with two final comments. The first has to do with its voting system. Australia is one of not many countries with compulsory voting. If you fail to vote you are subject to a fine. This puts voter turnout well above 90 per cent.[20]

Brought in back in 1924 by a Nationalist-Country Party coalition government, compulsory voting has not worked out obviously to bolster political parties of the left, as some might assume. If anything, for Reagan Republican–type reasons, compulsory voting may have been slightly to the advantage of the party of the right, though it is hard to know for sure.

One thing compulsory voting has done is to ameliorate the young-old phenomenon in countries with voluntary voting, where old people turn out to vote in much higher percentages than young voters and so – if you see the world in rather cynical public choice terms where self-interest overwhelms altruism – capture more of the middle-class churned welfare dollar. If that is a worry to you, compulsory voting offers the prospect of some relief.

On a more philosophical level, compulsory voting tends to stir the passions and evoke strong feelings. "Why should people who don't want to vote, or can't be bothered to do so, be compelled to do so and hence have the same say as I do?" That is the general grievance many people have when first exposed to compulsory voting. Certainly it was my first reaction. That said, after nine years now of living in Australia I have changed my mind and now favour compulsory voting. I think it can be defended, and preferred, on consequentialist grounds which is my default outlook.

The fact is that there are good outcomes associated with what some describe as the republican virtues of having interested citizens who take at least some interest in parties' policies and a modicum of responsibility for outcomes. It may not do much, but it does something to get more people involved (in an informed way) in deciding who will govern.

The overall cost-benefit calculation for compulsory voting now seems to me to score higher than for voluntary voting.

Whether you agree, or not, Australia combines that compulsory voting with a preferential voting system for its lower house of Parliament, the one from which the prime minister and Treasurer are drawn. Now only two countries in the world use a preferential voting system, sometimes know as ATV (alternative transferable vote) or AV (alternative vote). This system is much closer to the FPP system in the UK, United States, and Canada than to proportional systems used in continental Europe and New Zealand. Like FPP, ATV almost always delivers the "In Team" and the "Out Team" two-party majority government, with rare exceptions when small parties are the kingmakers, as in the UK at present. The key difference between FPP and preferential voting is that with the latter voters do not simply tick the candidate they favour; under ATV they need to rank numerically from first to last all the candidates. And no one wins until he or she receives the support of over half the voters in the district or constituency.

Think of it as an old-time political party conference where a nominee is chosen by having a series of ballots with the lowest scorer dropping off each time until someone gets the support of more than half the delegates. ATV is the same basic process only speeded up and done in one go. All the voters' first preferences are counted. If no one scores over 50 per cent the lowest scoring candidate is dropped and the second preferences of those voting for him or her are distributed. If no one is still over the bar then the remaining lowest person is dropped. This continues until someone gets over 50 per cent and wins.

Notice that this voting system lets voters opt for small parties or independents without wasting their votes. It measures who people dislike, not just whom they like. (So a voter who doesn't care who wins but really wants to throw the bums out and make sure candidate X loses has only to ensure X gets ranked last on his ballot.) And it means every elected legislator can say that he or she has the support of over half the district's or constituency's voters. Sure, they probably won't all be first preferences. Some will be second preferences, and on rare occasions even a few third preferences too. But this is more than winning candidates in the UK, United States, and Canada can say.

Combine those aspects of the voting system with a statutory requirement for constituencies or districts with the same numbers of voters, no more than plus or minus 10 per cent (unlike in Canada or the UK), and no gerrymandering (unlike most of the United States), and Australia looks very good indeed when it comes to the machinery that implements measuring what the majority wants. I would say that that electoral framework is better in Australia than in any of our other countries – and this without a bill of rights!

I finish this sketch of Australia by noting that it suffers from the same democratic deficiencies when it comes to treaties as the UK, Canada, and New Zealand (but *not* the United States). As in all Westminster systems treaties are entered into under the prerogative power, or straight out executive power, and do not need the approval of either or any house of the legislature. Put more bluntly, the democratically elected legislature can be bypassed.

This might not matter much as in theory these treaties are not considered to be part of the domestic law in the Westminster system. Alas, the judges not just in Australia but also in the UK and Canada and New Zealand have taken to interpreting statutes, and in some of them even constitutional provisions, in the light of these treaties. In effect, the treaties become – or influence – domestic law through the backdoor. This has had major impacts. For instance, it has significantly altered the federal balance of powers in Australia because the content of treaties was taken to augment the federal external affairs power and trump state power.

But appeal to international treaties and conventions by the judges is more insidious and undermining of democracy than just that. It is one of the causes of democratic decline I will be discussing shortly in part II.

In fact that finishes my sketch of the place of democratic decision-making in Australia. Now that we have done so for all five countries we have a sense of the baseline or measuring point for any claims about democratic decline. Each country starts from a different place as regards the role of letting-the-numbers-count majoritarianism in decision-making. But all five have seen that role decline in the last few decades, albeit to differing extents.

I turn now to the causes of that decline.

PART TWO

Causes of Decline

My claim in this book is that democracy is in decline. Yes, the rate of descent differs in each of our five countries. No doubt, too, none had the exact same commitment to letting-the-numbers-count, majoritarian decision-making as a baseline starting point. Yet whatever the individual starting points in the governing structures of the United States, United Kingdom, Canada, Australia, and New Zealand, the scope of democratic decision-making – and the extent to which it provides the final say over contestable and debatable disagreements of policy and principle in society – has gone down in all of them in recent decades. It has declined. The trend is the wrong way, at least if you are, like me, a majoritarian democrat.

In this part of the book I will chart the causes of that decline. I will do so under four headings or separate identifiable factors. Partly this approach makes the reader's task of following my argument easier. Partly, too, it helps us in attributing causation, or rather blame, for this unwanted democratic decline. That said, there is a cost to this approach of splitting causes into separate and distinct headings or categories. Put bluntly, the real world is messier and with more interconnected overlap than I will present it in this part of the book.

My four headings or factors in this second part of the book will be: Judges, International Law, Supranational Organizations, and Undemocratic Elites. Under each of these I will be pointing to further causes of this democratic decline, ones that can be lumped (or shoe-horned) under each main heading. As I said, this makes the argument easier to follow and the casting of aspersions more straightforward. Readers, though, need to remember that the causes of democratic decline are in fact all intricately interconnected, and in a way belied by a structure with four distinct and separate causes for that decline.

Take this as a caveat or warning then, that the picture I will paint in this part II of the book is inevitably – and unavoidably – a simplified one. Having noted that, let us move on to paint that picture.

JUDGES

A century ago in the developed common law world, which is more or less our focus in this book, judges were much, much less inclined to gainsay or second-guess the elected legislature. If we purge the word of all its sometimes pejorative connotations, we can say that as a rule the top judges were deferential to the elected branches.

Of course at that time women did not have the vote in the United States, UK, or Canada, though they did have it in the Antipodes. But if we come forward three or four decades, to just before the Second World War when women and men had the same voting entitlements, we still see that judicial deference. True, it was less evident in the United States – with its then virtually unique justiciable bill of rights – than in our other countries. But in all of them the judges deferred to the national legislature notably more than today.

In fact, if we put the United States to one side very briefly, we can say that the judges back then felt it illegitimate to gainsay or second-guess the elected politicians. Save mostly for federalism disputes in Australia and Canada,[1] where the unelected top judges acted as umpires deciding if a particular power to legislate lay with the national elected legislature or with the provincial or state elected legislatures (a power structurally much easier for letting-the-numbers-count majoritarians to stomach than any out-and-out power to invalidate statutes whoever enacts them), and the gainsaying and second-guessing was minimal. Parliament was supreme and sovereign in the UK and New Zealand; Parliament (within the limits of federalism and, in Australia, separation of powers concerns) came close to being so in Canada and Australia.

Of course none of that is to deny that in any of our five countries the judges had room to manoeuvre when interpreting laws (or constitutions). As we all know, and as will become plainer still by the end of this section, the power to interpret and so to ascribe meaning to the words used when the legislature makes laws should never be underestimated. At the point of application the person or persons with authoritative power to determine meaning often can make plausible cases for more than one reading or outcome. Often this will be due to ambiguity or vagueness in the legislative enactment. Other times the law will build in a value judgment – think of a law specifying that children of divorcing parents have their future arrangements determined "according to the best interests of the child" – whose application is inherently contestable and debatable and over which smart, reasonable, even nice people will differ and disagree.

In all these instances judges have a sort of law-making power. Think of it as an interstitial or gap-filling or ambiguity-resolving or value-opting power. This, of course, is inevitable in any system that relies on general written-down rules. It will give some measure – not an unbounded or wholly unconstrained or limitless measure – of flexibility, to the point-of-application judge. The alternative (which is to send all such cases of ambiguity, of vagueness, of further need for value judgments back to the legislature) is simply too inefficient and cumbersome.

Conceding that, of course, is not to concede that the amount of such flexibility and discretion conferred by how a law is drafted is unimportant. It can be very important indeed. In fact, many would argue, me included, that we ought to try to keep such discretion enhancing flexibility to a minimum by cutting down in our legislative language and wording on vagueness, ambiguity and the implicit abdication of moral judgments to those at the point of application.

Try as we might, though, to minimize these things, we will never eliminate them completely. That is just a fact of humans being limited biological creatures, language being a tool that deals in generalities, and humans disagreeing in core ways over any number of moral and value judgments.

So we should remember never to under-estimate the power of interpretation. And that is true, as I hope I have made clear, even when the task is being undertaken in good faith. It multiplies exponentially when the point-of-application judge decides he or she wants a particular outcome and then supplies the reasoning after the fact in order to get to that answer. That is bad-faith interpreting, or lying about what you really believe is the actual meaning of the words you are reading. And that is true however commendable your overall intentions (at least from your point of view).

I wouldn't think that anyone, with a straight face, could assert that that sort of bad-faith interpreting never happens, even in nice liberal democracies like the UK, United States, Canada, New Zealand, or Australia. The fact is that none of us can know for sure that what a judge says he's doing is in fact what he thinks he's doing. And it would be remarkable if no judge, ever, had indulged in this sort of "after the fact" or "ex post facto" fill-in-the-reasoning-that-gets-me-to-my-preferred-outcome approach. And not just today but fifty, seventy, one hundred years ago too. Greater judicial deference to the legislature back before World War II does not mean judges never ever lied about what they were doing. Justice Scalia of the US Supreme Court calls this kind of hypocrisy "the beginning of virtue,"[2] though we might also call it "the compliment that vice pays to virtue."

For our purposes I want only to be clear that when I say the judges back then were much less inclined to gainsay or second-guess the legislature, I am certainly *not* saying no judge ever did so. Even in systems in New Zealand and the UK where Parliament was supreme and sovereign, there would sometimes be just enough ambiguity or vagueness in the enacted law to achieve judicially desired outcomes, be it in good faith or bad.[3]

So my claims in this part of the book about the increasing willingness of judges in our five common law jurisdictions to override, circumvent, second-guess, frustrate, and gainsay the elected legislature are comparative and relative. Whatever the individual country's democratic starting point, the tendency of judges to do so has gone up. More so in some of our countries than others, but in all the trend is upwards.

With that in mind, let us move chronologically forward from the Second World War. In parts of the United States, of course, black Americans had no real or at least easy route to voting for two more decades. The same sort of claim could be made of Aboriginals in Australia. Democracy was improving in terms of making sure elections did not exclude certain groups – deliberately and intentionally exclude certain identifiable groups – from being part of the numbers whose voting views counted. All that was to the good, not part of a decline in democracy but rather an improvement. From the 1950s and 1960s onwards, however, we see judges become more adventurous or unconstrained by previous interpretive orthodoxies. As with so much when it comes to constitutions, constitutional law and constitutional interpretation, this starts in the United States and slowly (quite slowly) filters out to our other countries.

Over the next four or five decades judicial willingness to block or re-direct the views of the majority of voters, as expressed in laws passed by their elected representatives, increased noticeably. Or at least it increased enough for me to notice, to object, and to sit down to write this book.

At this point I could take the reader on a romp through a series of cases from the top courts in all our five jurisdictions, selecting my personal favourites in terms of hard-to-justify interpretive approaches that have the effect (intended or unintended) of enhancing judicial power. We might start with *Roe v. Wade*[4] in the United States, then move to *Baigent*[5] in New Zealand, the implied rights cases in Australia,[6] the *Alice in Wonderland*–mimicking *Ghaidan*[7] case in the UK (where the country's top judges asserted they now have the power when interpreting all statutes to read words in, read words out, ignore the legislature's clear and undisputed intentions, and do so even where there is no trace at all of ambiguity – not unlike Humpty Dumpty's claim that "a word means just what I choose it to mean"), and finish by picking at random just about any of the important Canadian Charter of Rights decisions,[8] so committed are the Canadian judges to living-constitution or living-tree interpretive approaches.

Analyzing these cases might even be of some modicum of interest to readers who are lawyers. Certainly I am not adverse to pointing out some of the implicit (and highly contestable) value judgments, the fast-and-loose playing with precedents and the assumptions that top judges – committees of ex-lawyers – have more highly developed moral (not legal, but moral) antennae than plumbers, teachers, hairdressers and even derivatives traders that pervade these cases.

However, I have resisted the temptation to descend into prolonged case analysis. I think that's largely of interest to lawyers, if it's of interest to anyone. So instead I want to be more general. I want to help readers see the main tools out there that can be used by those judges who do wish to inflate their own last word say at the expense of more majoritarian decision-makers. For the second-guessing and gainsaying judge, then, what are the devices and contrivances that help lessen the constraints on what answer she can plausibly give in a big case?

Expansive Approaches to Interpreting Legal Texts

How you are supposed to interpret a legal text matters. It matters a lot. And when that text is a written constitution, or a constitutionalized bill of rights (as in the United States and Canada), or a quasi-constitutional statutory bill of rights (as in the UK and New Zealand), it matters even more again.

Here's a crucial question. Are the words used in those constitutions and bills of rights locking the point-of-application interpreter into any outcomes, or are they the equivalent of a blank cheque telling that interpreter just to give it the meaning he happens to think is morally or politically best? Remember, these are words and phrases and terms that have been debated, argued over, sometimes fought over, always carefully tailored, and then put to some sort of vote. So at least in the time leading up to the adoption of these instruments and texts the people drafting them and the wider groups voting on whether to accept and institute them think the actual words chosen matter. They think they will provide constraints on what later-in-time interpreting judges can decide, on what they will allow them to do even as regards the striking down or rewriting of the elected legislature's statutes. From the vantage of someone living before the constitution or bill of rights becomes law, virtually no one thinks the text of these instruments amounts to nothing much more than a Spike Lee *Do the Right Thing* injunction to future judges who will have to interpret them and give them meaning and decide what they do, and do not, leave the elected legislature free to do.

Normally, of course, we all tend to think about how these important legal texts ought to be interpreted from the implicit vantage of a present day top judge. So we all hypothetically put ourselves in the shoes of these present day judges and ask what "without due process of law" or "right to free speech" forecloses the elected legislature from doing. And as almost no one is prepared to say openly and explicitly that these and similar entitlements place absolutely no constraints on the judge other than her own moral and political druthers – no external-to-her-own-sense-of-what-is-best limits on how she can decide – it follows that almost all of us believe the words actually used in the legal text have at least *some* constraining effect on today's interpreting judge.

But agreeing on that bare minimum still leaves it wide open just how constraining any particular approach to interpreting will be.

Some approaches, though, are likely to tie the interpreting judge's hands more than others. And if a lot of judges gradually shift from one approach to another, say from looking for the framers' original intentions and understandings to treating the document as a metaphorical living tree or living constitution, it may be that the effect of that shift has been to reduce the range and intensity of constraints on that judge.

I think something like that has in fact happened. One of the reasons democracy is now in decline is because judges have, by and large, shifted to an approach to interpretation (especially of bills of rights) that imposes fewer constraints on what they can say the words mean, and so gives them more latitude in gainsaying and overruling the democratic branches.[9]

Bear with me for a few pages now, because I think the best way to show you how this is at least a possibility – how this sort of living-constitution thinking reduces the external constraints on the interpreting judge – is to ask you to imagine the following scenario, one that shuns the vantage of today's top judges in favour of that of someone in the know back before the text was officially adopted.

So let's imagine the following hypothetical scenario. All of us are living in a New Zealand–style democracy, but one without any bill of rights. Let's call it "Krytarchia." We have majoritarian democracy. We have no written constitution. Our national record in terms of people being able to speak their minds freely, to associate with whom they wish, to practice their religion, as well as having comparatively liberal (for a democracy even) criminal procedure laws and approaches to dealing with suspected terrorists is clearly in the top dozen in the world. (By the way, that description would largely apply to Australia in my view, a country without a bill of rights. And it would even more so apply to New Zealand, bill of rights–free until 1990.) But the majority of voters in our hypothetical country, possibly due to the worldwide post–World War II triumph of American constitutionalism, now is hovering on the edge of adopting a written constitution for the first time ever, one with an entrenched, constitutionalized bill of rights.

Now think carefully about your and other people's expectations as your country Krytarchia ponders making this move. The new written constitution with its new bill of rights is *not* being imposed on you from outside after losing a war (think Japan or Germany). It's not the farewell gift of some departing colonial power (think most of Africa and chunks of Asia). It will come into being, if it does at all, only because people in Krytarchia, or rather some majority of them, want this change.

Another way of putting this point is that this new constitution and bill of rights will have legitimacy. Down the road, when judges are being asked to interpret its provisions, that legitimacy may matter. More specifically, that legitimacy in how it came into being may make it harder for point-of-application interpreters in the future to treat it and its provisions as shifting, malleable, not-locked-in things in need of updating, refining, widening, and rewriting by the judiciary.

Certainly from your point of view some time just before this new constitution and entrenched bill of rights gets adopted, you will think it has legitimacy once some majority, or super-majority, of your fellow citizens agree – even if you yourself are opposed.

You would also realize, if anyone bothered to ask you, that this constitution and bill of rights will not be self-interpreting and self-enforcing. Take the bill of rights. The various moral abstractions articulated in the language of rights cannot magically define themselves when it comes to how they will play out in any specific future line-drawing question that reaches the courts. (Think of cases such as whether "freedom of religion" means future legislatures cannot pass laws to ban the burkha in schools, or "right to free speech" will prevent them from passing defamation laws that value reputation highly enough to put the burden of proving truth on those being sued for publishing allegedly libellous words, or "right to a fair trial" will allow legislatures to soften or restrict the cross-examination of alleged rape victims by the accused's lawyer.)

Put it no more strongly than this. On the eve of going into this new set-up with a written constitution and entrenched bill of rights you and your fellow citizens of Krytarchia will realize that human judgment will be needed in deciding whether the guarantee against unreasonable searches and seizures, or the one assuring everyone of due process, does or does not result in some statute of the elected legislature being struck down, or even read down.

You will know before you embark on this journey that *some* interpretation will be necessary.

And with that realization comes another. It is this. Whether you support this move to adopt a written constitution with an entrenched bill of rights may well depend upon how it is likely to be interpreted. This is a key point to make.

Abandon the after-the-fact perspective of a top judge in a jurisdiction where there is already an established, powerful bill of rights that must be interpreted. Abandon it in favour of the vantage of a concerned citizen deciding whether such a bill of rights ought to be put in place. My claim here is that from that latter vantage none of the variants of living-constitution-type approaches has much appeal.

Tell a judge today that the rights in a bill of rights are best interpreted as broad and generous grants to those at the point of application to use their own moral and normative judgments and sentiments, in part at least, to determine how the rights best fit together, ought to alter over time or expand in line with the growth of some metaphorical living constitution or living tree, and from that judge's perspective that may well be quite palatable. From that point of view, talk of interpreting in a "progressive" way with its in-built assumptions about changing social values being the responsibility of unelected judges to update, cater to, and even genuflect before, is at its most attractive. Even from this vantage it is not a democratic scenario, to be sure. But the anti-democratic or countermajoritarian realities of this sort of approach to interpreting are fairly effectively hidden or disguised or pushed from view once you take up the standpoint – explicitly or implicitly – of one of today's top judges on the country's highest court.

By marked contrast, to put it lightly, the anti-democratic implications of the "this bill of rights has no real fixed content but is more of a handover or transfer to future unelected judges to update, alter and expand in ways *they* happen to think best fit with the document's most defensible overall understanding or with the most moral outcomes or anything broadly analogous to that" approach will be abundantly clear from the point of view of the concerned citizen back before adoption. In fact, make the implications of living-constitution interpretation plain, and I would bet few citizens of a democratic entity would vote for it before the fact. They would prefer no bill of rights at all – and hence the existing New Zealand–style status quo with all decisions in the hands of the voters – to this alternative where the fetters on majoritarianism are more or less up to the judges themselves, which is what living-constitution interpretation appears to deliver once its implications are made explicit.

One of the reasons for the decline in democracy, then, is that proponents of the ever-more dominant living-constitution approach to interpreting key constitutional provisions (including rights provisions) have forgotten how illegitimate and unattractive it would appear to anyone asked to endorse it *before the fact*. Just try it. Move to Australia where there is no national bill of rights and start lobbying for an entrenched bill of rights. And when Australians ask you how its rather vague, amorphous and indeterminate provisions (no abridging the freedom of speech or lack of due process, from the United States say, and the right to freedom of religion and to a fair trial, from the UK say, and to be equal before and under the law, from Canada say) will be interpreted by future top judges, you will be explicit. You will say the provisions will be interpreted in the light of international norms, of changing social values and mores, in order to keep pace with civilization, in order to ensure the document (whose words have been so hotly contested, negotiated and argued over) meshes with future treaties (ratified and unratified), paying more attention to systematic moral theories, context and diversity of felt experience than to any locked-in and unchanging meaning of the language finally used.

You wouldn't have a chance of getting anywhere near a majority of Australians to agree beforehand to anything remotely resembling that sort of interpretive approach, and we all know it. They'd laugh in your face. And were we able to ask voters, even now, in the United States, UK, and New Zealand, they'd hands down reject this interpretive approach too. (My native Canada may be an exception. I'd like to think not, but the infatuation with rule by judges there makes it harder to know.)

So what we have – one of the key drivers of increased judicial willingness to gainsay and second-guess the social policy line-drawing decisions of the elected representatives of the people – is an approach to giving meaning to fundamental legal texts that few people would agree to in advance. Up front it looks like an abdication of power to the judiciary, and an abdication at that whose extent is potentially always being pushed out and expanded and theoretically boundless.

This picture of majoritarian democracy being hollowed out and enervated by the interpretive choices of judges is not a necessary one. My claim is an empirical one. As I said, before the Second World War this expansionary interpretive approach was very uncommon, even in the United States. Moreover, one can paint quite a different (and considerably more attractive) picture to our concerned citizen in Krytarchia back before the decision has been made whether or not to opt for a written constitution and bill of rights.

That different picture would start by asserting that written constitutions, including entrenched bills of rights, are about locking things in. They are *not* vehicles for setting out a list of the country's most important values, no doubt in ways so abstract they finesse most disagreement. They are *not* meant to leave to future judges the changing and altering and providing of greater specification of that list as society "advances" and grows in accord with rather Whiggish presuppositions, and with more concern given to getting the upgrades right (according to the judges, that is) than to who can legitimately make them. No, we are locking in a particular set of arrangements. Our new constitution is about relative inflexibility, in the sense of demanding that supermajoritarian hurdles needed for constitutional amendment be passed before these particular provisions can be changed. That is why we argue and fight and debate over every word, and phrase and comma.

This same locking things in view goes for the bill of rights, too. If you vote to adopt one, we tell our concerned Krytarchian citizen, you are putting in place – no, locking in place – a particular set of protections. They will constitute a new floor-level set of protections. But above those floors things will be decided, as now, by means of majoritarianism and voting. We are not asking you to hand the judges ever expanding scope to strike down the legislature's laws. These enunciated rights will be floors, possibly new and higher floors than before. But they are in no way meant to cover all of society's future moral disagreements – think of euthanasia, abortion, same-sex marriage, capital punishment – by translating them from political disputes into legal ones.

Notice how this picture offers up a halfway house. Above our new floor-level protections we are deciding whether or not to put in place you will have wide-open New Zealand–style majoritarianism. If you dislike the moral views of the majority up there above these floors, you work to change those views. You do not get to cry "tyranny of the majority" and run to some committee of ex-lawyers to have them impose your minority moral judgment on to the preponderance of your fellow citizens. That is not what you will be buying with this constitutionalized bill of rights. In a democracy with voting we are all sometimes on the losing side of votes, but that doesn't make the victors part of some majoritarian tyranny.

Many years down the road then, if enough citizens of Krytarchia today opt to go down this route, you may find you have a one- or two-century-old bill of rights. Now if this rather old instrument locking in certain protections and guarantees turns out *not* to protect access to abortion or ensure same-sex marriage or prisoner voting entitlements, nothing, anywhere, will prevent the elected legislature from doing so by means of an ordinary statute. There will be no need to amend the constitution. Just get half your fellow citizens to agree and then legislate for the changes you (but not all others) happen to think are morally or politically mandated or optimal.

That's a process otherwise known as democracy. And so if, all those years down the road, some citizen is aggrieved because abortion has not been extended or same-sex marriage enacted or the treatment of suspected terrorists not generous enough, his grievance will be with the elected legislature and the voters. And his efforts for change will focus on the political process, not the courts.

As I suggested, this picture looks much more attractive to anyone taking up the vantage of someone having to decide whether to give up legislative sovereignty (the legally unfettered elected legislature) *before* the decision has been made. From that pre-commitment vantage all the talk we hear surrounding living-constitution interpretation is thin gruel. Why, in advance, would any democrat offer such unspecified powers to future judges constantly over the coming years to alter and change and no doubt, as well, to expand the coverage these protections provide – without the words agreed upon ever changing and without anyone ever having to go to the bother of seeking a constitutional amendment? Is this person betting judges' values and views, over time, will be more like hers than those of voters at large?

I repeat, then, that at the time you were attempting to get a bill of rights or written constitution itself adopted this "locking things in" understanding of what a written constitution is meant to do would be vastly more attractive than living-constitution notions. My opinion is that there would be few buyers, in advance, for the sort of interpretive approaches to rights-based instruments and texts largely on display today in Europe, Canada and among some of the top US judges. It is these approaches that are partly to blame, in my view, for the decline of democracy.

I go further. I say that all these instruments are sold to people on the implicit basis that something is being locked in – that any future extensions to rights will have to come either democratically by legislation or by constitutional amendment, and *not* by some mysterious, ineffable process whereby judges will claim to be uniquely well-placed to intuit society's deep-rooted values and to know their jurisdiction's (perhaps even civilization's) sentiments on where to draw hotly contested lines over disputes ranging from euthanasia to terrorist detention to same-sex marriage. That is how they are sold because the living-constitution approach simply could not be sold up front. Not in advance. Not in Australia. Not in the UK. Not in the United States. Probably not in any of our countries.

Of course thirty or forty years ago one could sell a bill of rights, in good faith, on the basis it would be locking in certain outcomes. You could work to put in place a bill of rights back then while honestly believing latter-day judges would interpret it in a way that locked in many outcomes flowing from all the negotiating and bargaining over which phrases and terms would, and would not, actually be included. Anyone trying to sell that claim today – as some bill-of-rights proponents in Australia are trying – cannot really be acting in good faith. We know from recent experience that Canada's top judges, almost immediately once their entrenched Charter of Rights was adopted in 1982, stated that it would be interpreted as a living tree, the meaning of whose provisions would grow and alter and blossom over time in conjunction with society's changing values and needs (etc., etc., etc., etc.). In Canada, in fact, the judges have been explicit and emphatic that interpretations not possible today (for instance, reading the rights to include an entitlement to welfare or government housing assistance) may become the correct interpretation in future, though the rights in the bill of rights will then have the exact same words. The words will remain unaltered, the meaning and reach attributed to them will change. Canada's judiciary is aggressively attached to ignoring the clear, undeniable understandings of those who drafted, negotiated and passed the Charter of Rights and just as committed to saying it is a document whose meaning will change over time. In fact, this orthodoxy is so strong in Canada that there are almost no dissenters among the top to middling ranks of the judiciary.

Imagine the response and lack of support for the Charter of Rights if this had been made plain before 1982.

Meanwhile we know that in the UK and New Zealand that their bills of rights, albeit both statutory, have also been interpreted with little concern for legislative intentions and understandings – at least as regards particular provisions rather than some grand, abstract claims about how the instrument as a whole was meant (allegedly) to make judges the guarantors of society-wide rights-respectingness.

Put it no higher than this. Canada, New Zealand and the United Kingdom provide little evidence that, once in place, the provisions of a bill of rights will be given the scope and reach that those drafting and approving it expected; nor that the limits on rights will be as expected; nor that how the rights interrelate will be as expected. More than anything, one would take from the interpretive experience of these countries that when you buy a bill of rights you are overwhelmingly just buying the rights-related views of future top judges – views that will pay homage to the document as some sort of metaphorically living thing, without ever pointing out that all the updating, altering, changing, rebalancing and everything else that takes place will be done by committees of ex-lawyer judges with next to no democratic legitimacy (in the thin, unvarnished sense).

Make that plain and explicit and it becomes a very difficult sell. That's what taking up the vantage of a citizen in a jurisdiction contemplating the adoption of one tells us. From that vantage the future lack of democratic input and legitimacy matters. Most people simply wouldn't sign up to these sort of externally unconstrained (or, if that's too strong for you, then comparatively less constrained) interpretive approaches.

Not only wouldn't they, they didn't. These approaches are judicial innovations. The democracy enervating consequences they bring with them are therefore the fault of the judges who adopt these approaches. And the present-day attractions of living constitutionalism, in my view, flow in large part from not making explicit to people that with these instruments in place they in effect are locked in by one of two things, either by the original intentions and understandings of people at the time of adoption (see the next subsection below) or by present-day judges' views. Both infringe on the scope for democratic decision-making, but the latter is considerably more worrying and carries with it a huge inflationary risk.

Let's return, for a moment, to the vantage of the citizen in a majoritarian New Zealand–type set-up contemplating whether to support a move to a written constitution with an entrenched bill of rights. As we have seen, she'll want to know how those documents will be interpreted. She is unlikely to want to opt for them if she is told – straight up and in advance – that they will be interpreted as living things that branch out and alter their meaning according to the understanding of future judges, and that the widespread majority understanding of the meaning of these terms that she shares is in no way being locked-in (subject to later constitutional amendment) or going to constrain what future judges can say they mean.

If you agree with that claim, consider a more specific variant. Ask yourself if anyone, when asked to support, say, the adoption of a bill of rights, would agree if he was told plainly, explicitly and without any finessing or artifice, that the meaning that would be given to various rights provisions would depend, in part, on what judges in other countries[10] with broadly comparable instruments thought theirs meant.

Knowing that a bill of rights limits democratic decision-making, by giving unelected judges power to gainsay and second-guess elected legislators, how many people would sign up in advance to one if they knew its meaning in future would depend partly on foreign law and the understandings of overseas judges? Or rather, would making this clear and certain increase or decrease the likely support for this bill of rights?

The usefulness of shifting our vantage from that of today's top judge (and, again, let me say that this is the vantage most of us implicitly adopt when thinking about issues of interpretation) to that of a citizen or framer back before one is in place is that the democracy-depleting effects of living-constitution approaches not only become clearer; they may well cancel the deal. You and he might be prepared to bargain away some democratic input in return for certain locked-in and unchanging limits on what future elected legislatures can do, limits articulated in the language of rights. However, the cost of the bargain may well become too expensive, may make too many inroads into the scope for democratic decision-making, if you know it will be interpreted in non-locked-in ways.

It gets worse, too. It gets worse because once it is made clear, in advance, that future judges will be looking overseas and appealing to foreign law to help themselves interpret the scope and reach of the various rights, and how they interrelate, and what limits on them are acceptable, and so when the judges themselves can and cannot strike down laws passed by the democratically elected legislature, opponents of such foreign law appeals will be able to marshal some devastating pragmatic objections.

To start, there are no hard and fast rules governing the use of foreign law and overseas precedents. Indeed, there are no rules at all.

Nothing like the notion of *stare decisis* – of adhering to the principles laid down in past decisions and not disturbing settled points of law – exists to help in choosing between the myriad overseas precedents on offer. There is nothing to guide the judges in determining when foreign law should (and shouldn't) be cited, which decisions should be cited, what weight those chosen should be accorded, and so on and so on.

Next, there is persuasive evidence from New Zealand suggesting that the citation of overseas authority in rights-based litigation leads to a gradual ratchet-up effect; that on average, over time, this practice results in judges extending and broadening the reach and ambit of various rights and the scope and range of their application.[11] Call this the ratchet-up effect.

Related to both of those is the cherry-picking temptation. This is the danger that judges will appeal to foreign law opportunistically, picking and choosing what they rely on or point to, and doing so only to reinforce conclusions that they wanted or intended to reach anyway. The simple fact is that there is a huge range of different opinions on almost all issues if you look to foreign law. Confirmation bias, or ignoring differing views, will be hard to resist.

One could even add to these the core level observation that overseas jurisdictions vary in comparative size and relative populations. For Americans, our four other common law jurisdictions of the UK (63 million), Canada (34 million), Australia (22 million), and New Zealand (4 million) have a *combined population* of just a little over a third of their population (318 million). These four are likely to be some of the jurisdictions most often cited by American exponents of appealing to foreign law, and not just because those who appeal to Zimbabwean or Sudanese precedents will be derided (as US Supreme Court Justice Stephen Breyer was when he referred to the law of Zimbabwe in a 1999 death penalty case[12]). But with a combined population a fraction of America's, why should the views – or even a consensus of views – of Canadian, British, Australian, and New Zealand judges count for any more than the views of Texan, Californian, or Floridian judges when it comes to the death penalty and whether that punishment is, or is not, a cruel and unusual one?

Someone less polite than I could make these points more harshly. We know the judges who interpret, sometimes or in part, by appealing to foreign law will not point to sharia law, say, to uphold the death penalty for apostasy or adultery or homosexuality, and this even though there are approximately a billion and a half Muslims worldwide, some two-thirds of whom polls show favour "a strict application of Sharia law in every Islamic country."[13] We know that won't happen because we know American, Canadian and British judges today – maybe not tomorrow, but certainly today – who are inclined to appeal to foreign law will be selectively mining only those overseas precedents and international tribunal decisions that throw up the generally mildly left-wing political standards and transnational line-drawing answers that they happen predominantly to find congenial.

So tell this to someone in advance, *before* a written constitution with its entrenched bill of rights has been approved by the majority of voters (remember, this hypothetical country is not one where these are being imposed on it just before decolonisation or after losing a war), and my assertion – and indeed my hope – is that that person would never agree to adopt these instruments knowing how they would be interpreted. Nor would anything near a majority of voters agree. No democrat would agree to such an open-ended blank cheque being handed to the judiciary. No one who thinks letting the numbers count and majoritarianism are the best ways – normally, even if not always – to resolve social disagreements bearing on contentious and debatable moral and political issues (whether translated into the language of rights, or not) and over which sincere, smart people disagree would agree to this in advance.

For American readers, we might go so far as to say that the naive transnationalism of US Supreme Court Justice Anthony Kennedy, as seen in the 2005 juvenile death penalty case of *Roper v. Simmons*[14] or the 2010 juvenile life imprisonment case of *Graham v. Florida*,[15] *as a method of interpretation*, would never get more than token support in advance. It is a minority taste par excellence, this sort of interpretive approach. And I say that as someone who likes the substantive outcome of *not* executing juveniles and *not* imprisoning them for life. I say that as someone who would work to get such laws off the statute book. But I would want that done through the elected legislature, *not* by judges using an interpretive approach that seems boundless and limitless in what it can do in the hands of a skilful and adept operator.

Would Any Different Interpretive Approaches Be More Constraining?

Let's say we do want an approach to interpreting important constitutional and quasi-constitutional texts that is more constraining on the judge than living-constitution-type approaches, with or without the added extra of cherry-picking overseas judicial decisions that point in the desired way. Are such options available? Just because we agree to a written constitution with its entrenched bill of rights on the premise we want – and think we're getting – provisions whose meanings are locked in and *not* shape-shifting, rather contentless will-'o-the-wisps merely expressing society's cherished and fundamental values in moral abstractions that finesse disagreement and revel in indeterminacy is not enough. Wanting entitlements and guarantees whose reach, meaning and extent of coverage is locked in (or largely locked in even) does not automatically mean there is an interpretive approach out there that will deliver that outcome.

So the question now is which, if any, ways of interpreting might deliver what we seek or want. How do the alternatives to living-constitution interpretation score on this front?

Originalism, sometimes less kindly described as "ancestor worship," is the obvious place to begin our search. For those who want things to be locked in the epithet of "ancestor worship" will bother them not at all. It's just that certainty and definiteness provided by the actual intentions and understandings of real life people that they want. "If the provision is outdated, get rid of it or alter it through the amending formula," they will say, "not by judicial fiat." Get together the numbers to amend the words. And more often than that, just get enough voters to win the next election, because most constitutional rights are floor-level protections above which the legislature, if it wants to extend things (to provide extra criminal procedure protections, say, or wider possibilities as to who can marry or scope for euthanasia), can do so.

That means the taunt of "ancestor worship" misses its mark. All sorts of things are left to the elected legislature, even with a written constitution and entrenched bill of rights. Those locked-in floor-level things that have been taken off the democratic table, however, can always be changed by constitutional amendment (think of, say, the Nineteenth Amendment to the US Constitution and women's suffrage), admittedly a very tough supermajoritarian task. But that was the deal going in. If locking things in seemed unattractive, especially as regards a bill of rights, you could have opted for no written constitution (like New Zealand) or no bill of rights (like Australia).

Of course you might respond by pointing out that you, personally, never agreed to anything. Not this written constitution. Not this bill of rights. Nothing. Any imaginary social contract or written agreement supposedly entered into by you isn't worth the paper it wasn't written on.

That's all perfectly true. That's why the really important issue, the one that has real bite in the here and now, is how to interpret these legal texts. And from your point of view locked-in outcomes, even if they be dependent on the intentions and understandings of long dead people, may well be preferable to having meaning determined by the moral druthers or moral theorizing or normative best-fit views of a small handful of today's unelected top judges – who, ironically, resolve disagreements among themselves by voting: "five votes beat four" is the decision-making rule on top courts, no matter how morally moving, or inspiring, or chock full of references to rights-based international treaties or the writings of John Stuart Mill the minority opinions and judgments may be.

The alternative boils down to this: Do I want the inroads into democratic decision-making to come from the original intentions or understandings of long-dead people where those intentions and understandings are unchanging and when inapplicable, things are left to democracy? Or do I want the inroads into democratic decision-making to be amorphous, fluid, shifting, and ultimately tied to the perceptions of today's judges as to what keeps the documents "alive" and what the morally pregnant terms ought to mean, for the moment. Which option is most attractive or least bad? That is the question. And which makes a smaller inroad into democratic decision-making?

In an indirect way on page 46 I have argued that the locked-in alternative is better, or less bad, according to taste. If you were putting these options to people beforehand, as the way some proposed bill of rights or constitution would in future be interpreted, you could never, ever sell the living-constitution approach to enough people to have these instruments adopted. That was my claim above.

Now I'm asking what, if any, interpretive approach might put more constraints on today's top judges. And having brushed aside as misguided the chant of ancestor worship, I'm looking first at the approach to interpretation known as originalism.

Proponents of originalism say it does lock in outcomes. You interpret by reading "cruel and unusual punishments [shall not be] inflicted" and then seeking to determine what the framers of those words intended (one strand of originalism) or what a well-informed person at the time understood them to mean (the other strand of originalism). Because you, the interpreter, are searching for a matter of historical fact – what real-life people back just before or at the time of adoption really intended or really understood – you are locked in. There is an unchanging answer to this search for a matter of historical fact.

Of course your view as to what that answer is might change, perhaps because some new papers are discovered and authenticated providing new evidence of what people thought back then. But that is quite different from interpreting by appealing to today's moral understandings of these terms – or more accurately, your view of today's understandings, or more accurately still, the judges' view, or to be as accurate as possible, the majority of top judges' view – which is a standard that will produce ever-changing answers over time. A search for historical fact at least seems to offer the prospect of locked-in answers as to what is encompassed by "cruel and unusual." It appears to foreclose answering that by looking to see what people (or more probably, top judges) today in Europe think, or what your own best moral understanding of these terms is. The question becomes "what was the understanding of cruel and unusual back then?," which provides an external to your own moral views constraint. Back then if capital punishment did not fall under the aegis or meaning of these terms, then whether to use capital punishment or not today is up to the voters and their elected legislators. They can eliminate it, or not, as the majority sees fit. It is an issue to be resolved by majoritarian politics, at the state level in some jurisdictions and nationally in others. What was locked in was only what those terms were understood to enact, or intended to mean, back at the time of adoption.

That picture, as I said, leaves more on the democratic table, not least because the judges who use living-constitution interpretive approaches can always keep expanding and altering what falls under the aegis of "cruel and unusual" – taking more and more (and in theory, though not in practice, potentially even less and less) off the democratic table and so reducing what you and I and other voters get to decide by majority vote. It is that non-locked-in approach to reading fundamental legal texts, the way many judges today are approaching the task of interpretation, that is reducing the scope for democratic decision-making. That's one of the bases for my claim that democracy is in decline.

Granting that, it's still an open question whether my sketch of originalism above can deliver in practice what it promises in theory, namely more constraints on the interpreting judge. Can it lock in outcomes in a way a citizen back before adoption would have wanted before agreeing to put a written constitution and entrenched bill of rights in place?

Certainly originalism as an interpretive approach comes in for steady attack. Critics ask, if we are seeking framers' intentions, as a group, how can we ever know them? And don't the many proponents who support a written constitution or a bill of rights or even a specific foreclosure of "cruel and unusual punishments" do so on different grounds and with different views as to their coverage and extent?

Dealing with critiques such as that pushed one group of originalists to abandon the historical search for original intentions in favour of looking for the original public meaning of the terms back then. But did that answer all that many disputes? Was it anymore constraining? Was there enough historical evidence? With the amorphous moral abstractions in a bill of rights – say, "cruel and unusual punishments" – how constraining, exactly, is the original public meaning when brought down from the Olympian heights of such disagreement-finessing terms and applied to specific disputes?

Attacks also came from a different direction. What if the framers really did intend to abdicate these moral decisions to latter-day unelected judges? What if that was, as a matter of historical fact, what they intended when speaking of "cruel and unusual punishments." Just leave it to future judges to bring their moral sensibilities and perspicacity to bear in deciding what is "cruel" and what is "unusual" as far as a punishment is concerned – maybe that was the actual intention? Or to put it more in terms we have been pondering, what if the framers intended the concept of "cruel and unusual punishment" to be one that was *not* locked in and that would vary and mutate through time, its scope, reach and coverage to be determined by unelected judges?

Originalism wouldn't be much use in that case for anyone seeking an interpretive approach that locked judges in. Having conceded that, this last attack takes originalism on its own terms. It makes a factual historical assertion – that this is what the framers, in fact, really intended. And I think the evidence in the United States, and Australia (but somewhat less so in Canada as regards its 1982 Charter of Rights) is against that, indeed compellingly against that sort of claim. They didn't intend any such undemocratic, potentially unconstrained delegation at all.

As for the earlier mentioned attacks, on whether intention can be attributed to groups or known at all, and on how useful original understanding of, say, the literal meaning of vague, amorphous rights-protecting phrases might be in resolving all that many real-life disputes, my opinion (as to the ability of originalist interpretation to lock answers in and constrain today's judge) floats between mild optimism and regretful skepticism.

Without doubt it is preferable to living-constitution approaches, if only because it tries to lock things in, and because it narrows what can be appealed to. It may also inhibit adventurism by forcing some things out into the open under the name of "construction" rather than "interpretation." The more sophisticated it becomes in its intellectual tools and edifices, though, the more skeptics doubt it is sufficiently constraining. I hope it does lock many answers in. I'm just not sure how often it does.

What I will say, though, is that sixty, seventy, or eighty years ago an unarticulated, implicit sort of originalist interpretation did seem to produce less judicial gainsaying of the elected legislature, vastly less in fact.

There is one other approach to interpreting the entrenched bills of rights in written constitutions that I should mention because majoritarian democrats might find it alluring. On this approach the judge comes at all disputes with the working assumption that the elected legislature's enacted law is proper and not to be struck down. That's the strong presumption going in. Only if that law seems to fail a sort of "puke test," or make the judge want to vomit it is so obviously morally distasteful to him when held up against one of the rights protections, only then does he strike it down.

That sort of approach, not unlike what you might think American judges such as Richard Posner or O.W. Holmes bring to the table, has some appeal – especially if you find yourself doubting the constraining effects of originalism. Of course some particular law related to punishing that might make *you* metaphorically puke might not make *him* or *her* or *them* do so. This puke test is a judge-dependent test. It's a port of last call, a last resort, for those trying to constrain the power expanding proclivities of today's unelected judges.

Whatever you think about how best to restrain those people, the judges, who have the authoritative power to tell all the rest of us in society what the provisions in our written constitutions mean

– including the various provisions that express vague, amorphous and emotively attractive moral abstractions in the language of rights – my focus in this book is just to show this is a cause of democratic decline. Indeed, it is a big cause. I am not confident, however, of which route offers the best likelihood of reversing the inroads into majoritarian decision-making that slippery, metaphorically challenged or inapt interpretive approaches hand to judges, only that living constitutionalism has to be rejected and jettisoned.

But I am confident that today's judges are one cause of the decline in democracy. Many have become puffed up, have vaunteth themselves, such that voters and elected officials must suffereth long and beareth their own reduced corresponding scope for decision-making. We democrats do not rejoiceth in this trend.

New Bills of Rights in the Last Thirty Years

In this section we ignore the United States and focus on three of our other four countries. Yes, one of the big causes of democratic decline is our unelected judges and how they have taken to interpreting and giving authoritative meaning to fundamental legal texts. No one should be in any doubt that how judges are going about that task today – or rather how the vast preponderance are going about it in Canada, the UK, and New Zealand and how many are doing so even in the United States and Australia – is a major reason why the scope for majoritarian decision-making has shrunk in the last few decades. No one should ever under-estimate the power of interpretation, especially once it becomes acceptable to think this task is not simply the search for locked-in intended meanings and once metaphors about constitutional or quasi-constitutional texts being "alive" are swallowed whole.

We can be somewhat more precise in pointing to a cause for this more lax, more externally unconstrained approach to interpretation when we concentrate on Canada, New Zealand, and the UK, and put the United States to one side for a moment. We can do that because each of these three countries adopted or enacted a bill of rights in the last thirty or so years – Canada in 1982, New Zealand in 1990, and the UK in 2000 (if we count when it came into effect nationwide there).

In all three of these countries the new bills of rights were taken by the judges to be licensing them to have more say in social policy line-drawing decision-making.[16] Now, to be fair, the judges themselves wouldn't quite put it like that. They would characterize it more like this: "Now that there is a bill of rights in place it is the job of the independent judiciary to vet all laws for whether they are rights-respecting. We are the ones who will ensure, or at least have the main role in ensuring, that people's fundamental rights are protected and upheld."

How that would happen, though, depends on the sort of bill of rights that was put in place and the meanings imputed to its provisions. Only in Canada were judges given US-style powers to strike down or invalidate laws the judges felt infringed the enumerated rights. But in all three countries how judges went about interpreting – how they gave meaning to the bill of rights itself (and what it was understood to mean), as well as to all the enactments and laws of the elected legislature – was affected by the bill of rights.

In Canada, as I have noted, judges gained a US-type power to invalidate legislation on the basis that it contravened one or more of the enumerated rights in the Charter of Rights. But as we saw above, rights do not interpret themselves. And as we also saw above, the Canadian judges wasted no time at all in announcing they would be interpreting these new rights in the Charter in a way that was in keeping with understanding the Charter as a living tree that would, over time, grow and alter and branch out in keeping with changing social values and needs.[17]

What follows from that, but what was virtually always left unsaid, was that it would be the judges – and only the judges – doing all this altering, changing, ramifying, recalibrating, and expanding (because there is a dearth of any pruning going on). They would be the ones who decided if, and when, the meaning of the rights would change.

Related to that, and also left unsaid, was that when the Canadian judges decided they would give some right or other an expanded, new meaning, and so a greater scope or extent of coverage and applicability, that also would have the inevitable effect of reducing the democratic pie in Canada. The more the rights were re-sized or even super-sized up by the judiciary, the fewer matters that would be left to be decided by the elected representatives of the voters.

This living-tree approach to the newly entrenched Charter of Rights gave the judges the basis for striking down and invalidating laws passed by the elected legislature related to who can vote, who can advertise and where (more particularly about tobacco), who can come to the country (or at least how those trying have to be treated), who gets covered by a province's human rights legislation, whether the legislature's compromise position on abortion can stand (again, no prizes for guessing this one), and also whether an elected government is able to freeze the salaries of judges as part of a general province-wide freeze of public servants' pay (to ask this one is to know the answer). Although it was more a common law invalidation, the Canadian judges even recalibrated who can marry (no prizes for guessing whether the judges' views were more in favour of same-sex marriage). And that's just a taste. I ignore the criminal procedure and exclusion of evidence rulings flowing, at least in part, from this living-tree understanding of what the rights cover (for the moment).

In fact, in one case to do with whether convicted and incarcerated prisoners must in all cases be allowed to vote, the Chief Justice of Canada said something telling. She referred obliquely in her judgment to countries that disagreed with her court's 5–4 striking down of legislation stopping the most serious criminals from voting while in prison, countries such as New Zealand, the United States, the UK, and Australia as it happens. The Chief Justice obliquely referred to these countries as "self-proclaimed democracies."[18] (Yes, that is a quote from her official judgment.)

Now perhaps I should pause for a moment and allow fully to sink in the staggering self-assuredness – no, the out-and-out moral sanctimoniousness and self-righteousness – of the top Canadian judge calling the UK, Australia, New Zealand, and the United States "self-proclaimed democracies"? What would have been the reaction if George Bush had said that? (Don't answer the last question. It was a rhetorical one. We all know what the reaction would have been.)

Let's leave aside instances of puffed-up judges and simply note this about Canada. Bringing in an entrenched, constitutionalized bill of rights that gives judges the power to strike down and invalidate laws passed by the elected legislature, as happened there in 1982, will always reduce the scope for democratic decision-making; it will transfer some social policy line-drawing power from the elected branches to the unelected judiciary. That is an inescapable part and parcel of choosing to have such an instrument as part of your country's constitutional arrangements.

But knowing you're transferring *some* power to judges by opting for this Charter of Rights does not mean you know, or suspect, or would ever agree to the amount that living-tree interpretive approaches shift to the judges. Put more bluntly, the 1982 Charter of Rights in Canada doubly reduced democracy. It took off the "for majoritarianism to decide" table what any locked-in understanding of a bill of rights would remove. But then, after it was in place, the judges unilaterally further increased their own share of the pie by announcing they would be interpreting this new Charter of Rights as some sort of living tree whose ambit, aegis, reach, and scope would be in constant flux, altering to keep pace (as it were) with civilization – or, to be more accurate, with the judges' own majority view (ironically) of what is most in keeping with civilized behaviour or changing social values.

From the vantage of a Canadian citizen back in 1982 this interpretive approach announced by the judges themselves not only magnifies the democratic deficit for future generations, it also happened without much of a democratic warrant for bringing in a Charter of Rights in the first place. There were no referenda or plebiscites in Canada on whether to have it; there were no elections, federal or provincial, on whether to have it; indeed, the election that brought in a prime minister later committed to bringing it in was fought on the price of gasoline.

That is Canada's bill of rights, the most US-looking one of all the rest. Despite quite a bit of self-congratulatory back slapping about the Charter of Rights in Canada it is not a bill-of-rights model that has been exported well. As we have seen in part I of this book, the section 33 notwithstanding clause attempt to restrain judicial power by making some judicial decisions subject to temporary legislative trumping has proved to be a bust, of no practical use in ameliorating American-style judicial supremacy and countermajoritarian effects. Indeed, as I speculated above, it may even have had the unintended effect of accentuating judges' willingness to gainsay and overrule the elected branches by giving them this fig leaf of supposed democratic legitimacy and cover to point to.

So the Canadian model has not been an export success story. Certainly some of its central tenets have been shunned in New Zealand and the UK. In fact, proponents of a bill of rights in New Zealand began by mooting an entrenched, constitutionalized Canadian-style bill of rights. How this was supposed to happen in a country without a written constitution was never made clear, but opposition to the proposal forced a semi-backdown anyway. The constitutionalized Canadian-style bill of rights was explicitly rejected in favour of a statutory bill of rights – in other words one that was passed by the legislature in the regular way and hence capable of being repealed and gotten rid of in the exact same way, by simple majority in the legislature.

Even that concession was not enough. In order to get the mooted statutory bill of rights through the left-wing Labour Party government caucus, and then enacted into law, two further changes had to be made that seemed to weaken this bill of rights considerably. First off, those pushing for a New Zealand bill of rights had to remove a wide-ranging remedies clause in the draft bill, one that authorized the courts to redress judicially perceived violations of rights by granting "such remedy as the court considers appropriate and just in the circumstances."

Removing completely that remedies provision still wasn't enough. More had to be done if this was going to get through Parliament. A new provision had to be added to the statutory bill of rights, one that explicitly stated that all other statutes, past and future, would trump this new bill of rights. Here's the provision, section 4 of today's New Zealand Bill of Rights Act. Have a look at it for yourself:

> 4. Other enactments not affected – No court shall, in relation to any enactment (whether passed or made before or after the commencement of this Bill of Rights), –
> (a) Hold any provision of the enactment to be impliedly repealed or revoked, or to be in any way invalid or ineffective; or
> (b) Decline to apply any provision of the enactment – by reason only that the provision is inconsistent with any provision of this Bill of Rights.[19]

On the face of things, this is as emasculating a provision as one could imagine. "All other laws, old and new, beat this one," it says. Yet even with that and the specific removal of the remedies provision, and the prime minister at the time's explicit assurance in the legislature during the bill's passage that this "Bill [of Rights] creates no new legal remedies for courts to grant. The judges will continue to have the same legal remedies as they have now, irrespective of whether the Bill of Rights is an issue" – even with all that it only managed to become law on a party political basis with every single member of the opposition party voting against it.

Yet almost immediately upon its coming into law the top New Zealand judges started upgrading it. The president of the highest domestic court, in the first ever Bill of Rights case to get that far, suggested that this new instrument (with its reading-down provision that I will mention below) may require courts to depart from long-established judicial interpretations of the meaning and intent of particular statutory provisions. Wow! Soon thereafter this same top New Zealand judge said in a different case that the new statutory bill of rights requires development of the law where necessary, with the goal of living up to international standards and keeping pace with civilization. (That's a quote.[20])

Not a word was uttered about how all this would enervate democratic decision-making, though that won't surprise any readers.

After that the New Zealand judiciary in a big 1994 case known as *Baigent's Case* (or *Baigent*) simply read back in an ability for judges to grant remedies for perceived Bill of Rights infringements, and did so despite the undeniable fact that the remedies clause in an earlier mooted draft had had to be removed in order to secure the bill's passage through the legislature. The New Zealand judges simply ignored or dismissed the legislative history en masse, or at least did so whenever it was convenient and useful to do so.

What else? Well, the judges simply created or made up a new cause of action or basis for suing sounding in (or based on) a breach of this new Bill of Rights. And they have overwhelmingly – not completely but overwhelmingly – ignored that section 4 "all other statutes beat this bill of rights" provision.

All in all the New Zealand judges can be thought of as having taken the Clark Kent bill of rights they were given by the democratically elected legislature and done all that they possibly could to transmogrify or reconfigure it into a Superman bill of rights.

That said, the New Zealand judges did not venture into *Alice in Wonderland* outcomes. They have stayed sane when it comes to the essential feature of statutory bills of rights, the thing that makes them far more potent and far more democracy-infringing than they appear on the surface.

Readers in the United States and Canada will take it for granted that a bill of rights allows judges to strike down or invalidate laws whenever the judges decide some law infringes one or more of the moral abstractions (written in the language of rights – think "right to free speech" or "no unreasonable search and seizure") in the bill of rights. They take it for granted, in other words, that it is that striking down power in the hands of an appointed judiciary that causes what Americans rather quaintly refer to as "the countermajoritarian difficulty."

Now statutory bills of rights simply do not let the unelected judges do that. Judges cannot invalidate the laws passed by the legislature. But that's not the end of the question. Statutory bills of rights such as the ones in New Zealand and the UK contain provisions known as reading-down provisions. They direct the judges to do whatever they possibly can to read all other laws in a rights-respecting way. And that little mandate or directive at the heart of these statutory bills of rights, what I've labelled as a reading-down provision, has the potential to turn a statutory bill of rights into a constitutional US-style one, at least as far as giving power to judges and eating into the scope for democratic decision-making is concerned.

Think of it this way. Suppose judges read the UK version ("So far as it is possible to do so, legislation must be read and given effect in a way that is compatible with [the enumerated] rights") or the New Zealand version ("Whenever an enactment can be given a meaning that is consistent with the rights and freedoms contained in this Bill of Rights, that meaning shall be preferred to other meanings"). And suppose, too, that judges opt to take such reading-down provisions to be Spike Lee–like licenses "To Do the Right Thing." How close could they come to interpreting "between a man and a woman" to mean, say, "between a man and a man," or "no full cross-examination of alleged rape victims" to mean, say, "yes full cross-examination" or "black" to mean "white"? Put differently, could the judges use these reading-down provisions to rewrite or redraft statutes which they, the judges, considered to be deficient as far as respecting rights?

And if the judges did go down this road, ask yourself what the difference would be – in terms of the inroads made on democracy – between American and Canadian judges who simply invalidate disfavoured statutes and British judges who rewrite them. If anything, the former situation would be preferred by us majoritarian democrats on transparency grounds. We can see what is really happening. And on rule of law grounds. The statutes that weren't struck down would mean what they say they mean.

Of course perhaps this spectre of *Alice in Wonderland* interpretation in line with Humpty Dumpty's remark that "when I use a word it means just what I want it to mean" is just scaremongering. Perhaps these reading-down provisions don't in fact give rise to "interpretation on steroids" outcomes.

As I noted a few paragraphs back, the New Zealand judges have stayed sane. Yes, the statutory bill of rights there has increased their power at the expense of the legislature's. Yes, some political disagreements have been translated into the language of rights and shuffled off to the judges for them to resolve. And yes, the reading-down provision there has affected how judges give meaning to other laws; it has increased their discretion at the point of applying the legislature's laws, which is another way of saying it has upped their power.

But in New Zealand the reading-down provision has taken the judges only so far. They have stayed sane when telling us what it allows them to do.

By contrast, in the United Kingdom the top judges there seem not to have stayed within the bounds of sanity. Let me quote from the leading case in the UK, from their highest court, on what this reading-down provision allows (or the judges themselves say it allows) them to do. And remember, when reading these quotes from the *Ghaidan* case, that this was a 2004 decision. And remember that all the judges in that case agreed on this point about what the reading-down provision allowed them to do. And remember, too, that what they said in *Ghaidan* has been affirmed and affirmed and affirmed again.

Are you ready?

> It is now generally accepted that the application of s. 3 [the reading-down provision in their statutory bill of rights] does not depend upon the presence of ambiguity in the legislation being interpreted. Even if, construed according to the ordinary principles of interpretation, the meaning admits of no doubt, s. 3 may none the less require the court to ... depart from the intention of the Parliament which enacted the legislation ... It is also apt to require a court to read in words which change the meaning of the enacted legislation, so as to make it [bill of rights] compliant.[21]

Wow! Here are the highest judges in the UK prepared to state openly and explicitly, in an official judgment, that they can now interpret all other democratically enacted statutes in a way that "departs from the intention of the elected Parliament." They can do so when "the meaning admits of no doubt." They can "read words in which change the meaning of the law." By analogy, they can also read words out.

Forget concerns about democracy, as blatant and troubling as they are after reading such assertions. What about the rule of law, in its old-fashioned sense that citizens should be governed by general rules whose content they can know in advance and so adapt their conduct accordingly? After *Ghaidan*, and the judiciary's claims about what they can do now that the statutory bill of rights' reading-down provision is in place, no UK citizen can know for sure what any statute or law requires of her – no matter how clear the words, no matter how lacking in ambiguity or indeterminacy – until the highest judges have spoken and decided whether *they* will or will not rewrite that law to make it more in keeping with their view (or the view of the majority of them, ironically enough for us majoritarian democrats) of what the nebulous, amorphous rights provisions demand.

In fact, even after the highest judges have spoken, who can be sure they won't change their minds. Canadian top judges change their minds on rights issues. (What sort of advertising is protected by free speech is one of various examples.) So do American judges. And so will UK judges. That means the content of a law can never be known for sure by a concerned British citizen. Not while what the reading-down provision's command to the judges to do what is "possible" to interpret laws in a way that meshes with their own judicial (majority) view of what is rights-respecting is being understood in this almost boundless *Alice in Wonderland* way. In fact one of the top UK judges has said they can do anything up to the point of "judicial vandalism,"[22] whatever that means and whatever limit that might impose in practice.

Still think the UK judges, with what some people described before its enactment as "this harmless statutory bill of rights," are noticeably less powerful than their American and Canadian judicial colleagues? Still think a statutory bill of rights (which does not overtly and in plain view allow judges to strike down legislation and gainsay the elected branches) makes noticeably fewer inroads into democratic decision-making?

I don't. But if you do you might like to know that in later cases the top UK judges also described this "harmless little statutory bill of rights" as ushering in "a new legal order."[23] And you might be interested in hearing that another aspect of the UK statutory bill of rights, the one that allows judges when they aren't rewriting unambiguous laws to depart from the legislature's clear intentions to issue a Declaration of Incompatibility. This is an official declaration that some law is in breach of people's fundamental rights – though if it were aiming for factual accuracy it would have to be a more modest declaration that some law, in the opinion of a majority of the judges hearing the case, is not rights-respecting though the issue is highly contentious and debatable and no one has a pipeline to God as to who is correct in this situation of smart, nice, reasonable people simply disagreeing.

Alas, the declaration glosses over such complications and just assumes that what the judges (or, rather, the majority of them) announce about rights is to be taken as authoritatively correct and indisputable. At least that has been its effect in the UK. More than two dozen such declarations have been issued by the judges – and recall that these are technically just announcements of what the judges think, which legislators could in theory ignore – and every single time without a single exception the legislature has deferred to the judiciary. Once appeals have been exhausted, the legislators have changed the law to be in keeping with judicial opinions about rights. The judges have won, much as they do in Canada despite their section 33 notwithstanding clause.

Now if there are still readers who think US and Canadian judges are vastly more powerful than their British counterparts, just be aware that Oxford legal academic Aileen Kavanagh (who likes bills of rights and likes powerful judges) thinks the same as I do, a majoritarian democrat, when it comes to how potent this supposedly harmless little statutory bill of rights has proven to be. Kavanagh thinks it is tantamount to a US- or Canadian-style entrenched bill of rights and that judges exercise strong form constitutional review powers when operating and interpreting it.[24]

For our purposes in this book we need only go as far as this. Statutory bills of rights reduce the scope for democratic decision-making. They increase the power of judges just as the US-style Canadian Charter of Rights did. No doubt the decline of democracy has been more pronounced under the UK's statutory bill of rights than under New Zealand's,[25] but then I am not alleging any uniformity in the rate of decline across our five countries. My claim is simply that democratic decision-making is being eroded, that what is left to be resolved by letting the numbers count is shrinking, in all five of them.

And in this section I have tried to show the reader how the comparatively new bills of rights in Canada, New Zealand, and the United Kingdom have played their parts in that decline. They have increased the power of the unelected judiciary. They have done this in part by giving judges a new role as overseers of what the elected legislature is allowed to produce, as in Canada. But these instruments have also altered how judges read the statutes produced by the legislature; this has happened in the UK, New Zealand, and Canada; it has had the effect of diminishing the range of issues left to majoritarian institutions to resolve. And these bills of rights have even been the catalyst for judges to tell us that they will interpret the bills of rights themselves in a living-tree or living-constitution way, whereby over time the unchanging words enunciating the rights get assigned new meanings with more scope of coverage as time goes by. And that too has negative implications for partisans of democracy.

So here is yet another way in which judges can be seen as a cause of democracy's decline. How these judges are chosen surely matters then.

Let us finish this section on the judges' role in bringing about democratic decline by considering whether the appointment process for judges can itself enervate democracy, at least in some of our chosen countries.

How Judges Are Appointed

We finish cause number 1 of democratic decline – namely, the judges – by looking briefly at how they are chosen.

Let me start by recounting the typical attitude of Canadians, New Zealanders, Brits, and Australians to the way top judges are appointed in the United States to their Supreme Court and Federal Courts. That typical attitude is one of disdain, verging sometimes into a rather smug condescension. And that attitude is widespread not just among lawyers and judges in these Commonwealth countries, it is prevalent, too, among elected legislators, newspaper columnists, and what might be termed "educated opinion" generally.

And it is wrong! In a world with ever-more powerful judges there is much to be said for the openly political way in which America's top federal judges are selected. There is much to be said for the Senate confirmation process, with its grilling of presidential nominees and its potential for voting down the candidate nominated.

Once judges have the considerable power that goes with being able to strike down and invalidate laws enacted by the democratically elected legislature (as in Canada and the United States) or being able to rewrite those laws to produce what they, the judges, happen to think is something more rights-respecting (as in the UK and New

Zealand), then majoritarian democrats will care very much how those judges are chosen. If judges who are in no way directly accountable to the people do now have these extra powers – powers they certainly did *not* have forty years ago in any of our Commonwealth countries – then we should look carefully at the way the American system at least provides for an element of majoritarian input into who gets these jobs.

Notice that the American system of appointing Supreme Court and other top federal court judges makes nominees appear before a committee of elected legislators (from the upper house Senate). Having probed nominees this committee can stall nominations indefinitely (though for the very highest Supreme Court nominees this is not politically possible); it can also let their nominations go forward to a full vote of the Senate where nominees can be, and have been, rejected. In other words, you only get to be a top federal judge in the United States if a majority of elected legislators from the Senate vote for you.

In the United States this political job – and we can argue about *how* political judging is or isn't but *not*, with a straight face, that this power to strike down or redraft statutes is entirely free of political considerations or that one's underlying moral and political judgments and sentiments never enter into how one decides on the bench – requires those selected to pass an openly political, majoritarian hurdle. Sure, the criteria brought to bear by the voting Senators will not be simply whether the nominee is from the same political party as they are or whether this is the candidate they would have chosen. But politics will enter into whether each Senator votes to confirm or not.

It is this overt politicization of the judicial selection process that gives rise to the disdain and smug condescension in Ottawa, London, and Wellington. (Canberra we can consider an outlier on this issue, as we shall see, not least because lacking a national bill of rights Australia's judges have less scope to gainsay the elected legislature.) In those capitals and beyond they tut-tut and decry the spectacle of nominees being asked about their views on abortion, same-sex marriage, how best to interpret a written constitution, whether it can be considered in some metaphorical sense alive, what role empathy should play, not to mention their having to field questions about their past personal behaviour and decisions when law deans or lawyers.

The basic complaint from the "isn't this an awful way to pick your judges" brigade is that with this sort of probing, questioning and public exposure many good candidates will not put themselves forward or accept a nomination. That's the basic claim or gravamen. But there seems next to no evidence in support of it. American Supreme Court nominees and appointees seem at least as accomplished and smart as their British and Canadian counterparts. Nor is there any shortage of people who are prepared to undergo this confirmation process. Indeed, so attractive do some people find the prospect of a top judicial job that they are prepared to have their candidacy remain in limbo, stalled over objections to them, for months and sometimes years.

So a powerful and blunt response to those who say that the American way of selecting judges keeps all or many of the best people from putting their names forward is just to deny there is any factual basis to that claim at all. Plenty of excellent candidates seem prepared to pay this price, and more.

Of course even if some few potential would-be judges were discouraged by this US-style Senate confirmation process, one would still need to ask whether those negatives and costs would be outweighed by the benefits of democratic input and transparency and implicit public recognition that these top judges are, in part, political actors. I think the answer to that, for me and for any majoritarian democrat, is "yes."

Not all critics of the American system restrict their worries to whether some good or excellent candidates will be deterred from seeking judicial office. It is not just concerns tied to the merits and talents of those ultimately appointed as top judges that motivate their dislike of the American system. Some simply do not wish the essentially political nature of the judiciary's job under a bill of rights to be openly admitted. They would prefer this to stay in the closet, out of sight as much as possible. They want the trappings of an apolitical judiciary without the reality any longer of that sort of judiciary actually existing.

Let me explain that last claim. One of the typical responses one hears from defenders and supporters of bills of rights (be they US- and Canadian-style or UK- and New Zealand-style) is that the unelected judiciary in fact has a modicum of democratic legitimacy given that it is appointed by the elected executive. Now this sort of claim, as we have seen, has some force in the United States. There, not only are the nominations made by an elected president, those who are nominated also have to be confirmed by the elected upper house of the legislature.

For majoritarian democrats like me this is still a matter of second best, of injecting an element of indirect democracy into a set-up with very powerful judges indeed. Yet if a good many of society's contentious and debatable social policy line-drawing decisions are going to be made by unelected judges, by committees of ex-lawyers, then US-style democratic input into who gets these jobs is preferable to a lack of such input.

And therein lies the core conceit, or perhaps deceit, of all those in Canada, the UK, and New Zealand who look down on and disparage the American system for appointing top federal judges. What you have today in those three Commonwealth countries is one side of the US equation but not the other. You have the powerful judges, yes, but much less democratic input into how they are chosen.

It wasn't always so unbalanced. Absent an American-style appointments process, these three Commonwealth systems could traditionally claim that unelected top judges were at least appointed by the elected prime minister and Cabinet. True, there was no legislative vetting of the choice made by the executive. But it was still the case that the unelected judge was being selected by the elected official.

Now forty, or even thirty-five, years ago this traditional Westminster system of judicial appointments was arguably preferable to the American system. Why? Well, given that no bill of rights was then in existence that handed extra moral and political line-drawing powers to the judges and it was abundantly clear, comparatively speaking, that the judges would defer to the elected Parliament on contentious moral and legal issues. They would defer even when those issues were articulated in the language of rights. The equation was in fact balanced back then because outside the United States the judges were much less powerful. There was no need for a second-best form of democratic input into how judges were chosen, namely appointing them along US lines.

So thirty-five or forty years ago in our Commonwealth countries it was comparatively easier to select judges on technical legal expertise grounds with a fair degree of insouciance about the fact the nominee does not share the political and moral views of the appointer. Indeed, this appointing of those known to be in the opposite party's political camp happened regularly. However, introduce a bill of rights in Canada in 1982 or New Zealand in 1990 or the United Kingdom from 1998 and that comparative insouciance disappears. The values of the appointee matter, not just his or her technical merit as a lawyer.

At that point, because a bill of rights has come into play and significantly altered (that is to say, increased) the authoritative powers of unelected judges to resolve debatable, contentious social policy issues, I think the American appointments system becomes preferable to the traditional Westminster one. It doesn't rebalance the equation, at least not for majoritarian democrats, but it does add a bit of democratic oomph to the scales in the form of an open, public confirmation system run by one of the two elected Houses of the legislature – one that can and does sometimes veto the choices made by the executive.

Let me put it this way. Some who voice disdain for the way top federal judges are chosen in the United States want to have their cake and eat it too. They want the more powerful "countermajoritarian" judges who can second-guess and gainsay the elected branches of government but they do not want to employ a system for appointing such judges that admits such judges have become more politicized and puts in place a few checks and balances on their newfound (and countermajoritarian) powers.

In the absence of a bill of rights, then, I think one can powerfully defend the traditional Westminster or Commonwealth way of appointing top judges, where this power simply lies in the hands of the elected executive with no check in the hands of the legislature. Bring in a bill of rights that significantly boosts the point-of-application powers of unelected judges, however, and majoritarians will think the US system better, or at least less bad.

Of course saying that – that with a bill of rights in place the US method of appointing judges beats the traditional Commonwealth method – does not rule out the possibility that the traditional appointments process might be made worse, not better. It does not rule out the sort of reform that moves the system in the direction of being even less democratic and having even less democratic input.

Alas, that is precisely what has happened, most notably in the United Kingdom. There, in conjunction with their new bill-of-rights empowered judges, they have also jettisoned the traditional appointments process in favour of one with no democratic input at all. Even the enervated and insipid claims that bills of rights have an indirect democratic warrant or pseudo-legitimacy given that the judges operating them have been appointed by the elected executive, even those half-hearted claims on behalf of majoritarian democracy have been rent asunder by what has happened in the United Kingdom.

For majoritarian democrats like me it is deeply depressing.

Before I outline this new UK system for appointing judges that manages to squeeze out virtually all democratic input into who gets these jobs, let's take a moment to consider what options there are for anyone wanting to move away from the traditional Westminster Commonwealth judicial appointments process where the elected executive – the prime minister and Cabinet – have a more or less unconstrained power to pick whom they want.

First off, and perhaps ironically, the American-style appointment of top judges system is only an option in Australia – which doesn't need it because it does not have a national bill of rights and its top judges have much less discretion and ability to gainsay and overrule the elected legislature than in our other countries.[26] The traditional appointments process works fine in Australia.

To put in place a US-type appointments system you need to have real bicameralism, with an elected upper house not always under the control of the political party making the judicial nomination. You need that so that there is no guarantee a nominee will be able to make his way out of the confirmation crucible.[27] And of our four non-US Commonwealth countries, only Australia passes that test. As we have seen, Canada and the United Kingdom do not have elected upper houses. New Zealand does not have an upper house of any sort. That means that for these three countries there is no plausible way to mimic the US appointments process and bring in an extra dollop of democratic input into who makes it onto the top courts.

Incredibly though, at least in my view, the UK has moved in the other direction. Yes, they have jettisoned the traditional system where the elected executive is legislatively unencumbered in deciding who will sit on the top courts. But they have jettisoned that traditional Westminster appointments process for one with *less* democratic input. In fact it has virtually no majoritarian input at all.

Here's the new judicial appointments process the former Labour government in the UK opted to put in place some half dozen years or so after enacting their statutory bill of rights. (And note that the new Conservative-led coalition government has given no indication of wanting to change this.) It is a process that leaves the elected branches of government almost completely neutered in so far as appointing the unelected judges is concerned. And remember, these will be the judges who operate their *Ghaidan*-fuelled statutory bill of rights.

In the UK a Judicial Appointments Commission (JAC) now picks the top judges, with the Lord Chancellor (a Cabinet minister non-British readers can think of as a justice minister) having only a highly constrained power to reject the JAC's choice on the basis the person chosen "is not suitable for the office," or to ask the JAC to reconsider due to a lack of evidence that "the person is suitable." And the Lord Chancellor has to give reasons in writing for doing this.[28]

It doesn't stop there, this emasculating of any majoritarian input into who will be appointed as a top judge. You see if either of those above steps ("X is unsuitable" or "reconsider X because there's a lack of evidence of suitability") are taken by the Lord Chancellor then the same one cannot be taken a second time by the Lord Chancellor should the JAC decide to resubmit the same name. And at the next stage the Lord Chancellor simply "must accept the person selected by the JAC."

This new UK system for appointing judges may be many things, but what it assuredly is not is one that allows supporters of their statutory bill of rights to claim the judges operating it – whose powers have undoubtedly gone up vis-a-vis the elected legislature's – have even a modicum of democratic legitimacy. That sort of claim, whatever you think of its overall worth, is clearly open to Americans to make. In a less vigorous way it was open to make under the traditional Westminster Commonwealth method of picking top judges. It is emphatically and undeniably *not* open, though, to anyone in the UK today to make.

Quite simply, under this new UK system there is virtually no democratic input whatsoever into the appointment of judges. Next to zero. Zilch. Indeed, for those who are closet aristocrats in the United Kingdom, who prefer a strong aristocratic element in their jurisdiction's governing arrangements, this combination of a potent statutory bill of rights and a JAC for deciding who gets to be a judge satisfies that preference remarkably well – at least if ex-lawyer judges get to count as today's aristocracy.

The reader might like to know about the composition of this JAC. Well, the JAC has fifteen members, including five judges and two lawyers. That makes it a dead certainty, in my view, that appointed lay members will defer to the lawyers and judges. The newly created Supreme Court (the renamed or rebranded Judicial Committee of the House of Lords) has its own unique, just-for-it appointments commission, but it too is top heavy in legal members including the country's two most senior existing judges.

My view, my strong view, is that judicial appointments processes like those in the UK are highly suspect. No, that's too restrained. They are undesirable, awful and inherently undemocratic in all ways. In a world where unelected judges have become more and more and more powerful – in New Zealand, Canada, and the United Kingdom without doubt but elsewhere too in the democratic world, including in Australia – this sort of approach to choosing them has big dangers that massively outweigh the claimed benefits.

Start with those claimed benefits. Proponents of JAC-type approaches tend to try to sell them by focusing on the desire for an independent, apolitical judiciary. Put the power to pick top judges in the hands of some JAC-type committee and you will depoliticize who gets picked, or so goes this claim. The total lack of any democratic input into who ends up on the bench, if it concerns proponents at all, is a price they think worth paying to get this claimed depoliticized judiciary.

Such a claim, however, is rubbish. It doesn't stand up to any probing. It is only remotely plausible if one downplays or undersells the power a bill-of-rights transfers to the judiciary, say by ignoring what a *Ghaidan*-fuelled reading-down provision allows judges to do in the way of rewriting statutes they don't like (or, to express it the way they would, statutes that they have judged to be inconsistent with the broad, amorphous rights guarantees). The more the facts show judges prevailing over the legislature in rights-articulated disagreements, the more it matters (and not only to those on the losing side of such disagreements) who gets to be a judge. More to the point here, the more say judges have to resolve these rights-related social disagreements, the less plausible it is to think any judge – however appointed – can be apolitical or depoliticized. Making a choice involving taking sides on same-sex marriage or abortion or prisoner voting or capital punishment and all the rest is to make a political choice. Sure, the politics can be and have been translated into the language of rights and transmogrified, too, into a legal question. But that doesn't make the judge's choice on where to draw the line on these highly contested and at core moral issues somehow magically ones wholly divorced from that judge's world view and underlying values – and that's true even where the judge happens to be a member of that now seemingly disappearing species that will interpret a clear legal text as mandating an outcome that goes against his personal moral beliefs.

That means who is appointed matters. This person rather than that one may well change the outcome. In any real-life sense, that's politics. For majoritarian democrats, if you can't restrain the power of judges so that on all disagreements with the legislature (including rights-related ones) the unelected judges defer or lose, then a poor second-best is to have democratic input into who becomes a judge. The United Kingdom's JAC approach takes that away too.

Related to this almost total lack of democratic input into the appointment of judges is the not unrelated issue of self-selection or memes. Judges and lawyers have a big role on these JAC-type commissions. They make up just a shade under half of the members, but even at that level it is hard to believe appointed lay members will overrule judicial and lawyer members – ever, in any circumstances in which judges feel at all strongly.

The downside here is not so much the potential mediocrity of the JAC-appointed judges. The danger is much worse; it is of a narrowness of outlook and a lack of heterogeneity among those ultimately chosen. The fear is we will end up with an insulated, self-selecting lawyerly caste – mediocre or otherwise – whose views on same-sex marriage, abortion, euthanasia, how to balance criminal procedures and public safety and other contentious issues are noticeably at odds with the general voting public's. Nor is this a farfetched worry, as a moment's comparison reveals of the general views of most (not all, but most) New Zealand lawyers and legal academics as opposed to the public at large on, say, sentencing, capital punishment, same-sex marriage, and more. Or American lawyers versus the public at large. Or Canadian ones.

The same goes for the UK. This JAC-appointments process gives rise to a self-selecting lawyerly caste of judges there, judges with bill-of-rights powers to get their way against the elected legislature. This JAC process also makes it difficult for a political party that has been out of power for some time, but now has won an election, to appoint a judge from among those lawyers who hold minority views (for lawyers that is, they may quite possibly be majority views among the public at large).

Here's the bet proponents of a JAC-type regime are making. They're betting those on any appointments board will never fall victim to the temptation just uniformly to go with candidates who share broadly similar worldviews to their own, and so shun the Scalias, Posners, Thomases, and Roberts (to put it in US terms) however impressive their credentials.

Let me put my argument here no higher than this. Even if it could be done, and I say it could not, taking all the politics out of judicial appointments is not a self-evidently good thing. Indeed, once a bill of rights is in place it is, to the contrary, an out-and-out bad thing. For those of us worried about the increasing power of unelected judges in Canada, New Zealand, the United States, the UK, and Australia, and relatedly worried about the legalization of politics and of the ever-expanding settling by judges of rights-based disagreements in society, this sort of UK innovation for picking judges makes things worse, not better. It further diminishes democracy and settling contested social disagreements by counting everyone as equal and letting the numbers count.

Recap and Final Remarks on Judges

That finishes our cause number 1 for democratic decline in all five of the Anglo-American countries under consideration. That cause is the judges. Over the past forty-odd years their influence and power has grown, in some cases markedly, and it has grown at the expense of elected, majoritarian decision-making. This can be traced in part to the adoption by them of more expansive, less constraining (on them) approaches to how to interpret important legal texts, including the written constitution if one exists in that country.

Judges' inflated say can also be traced in part, in Canada, New Zealand and the UK, to the adoption of new bills of rights. Whatever else these instruments do they have undeniably increased the power of unelected judges and their ability to prevail in rights-articulated disputes with the elected branches.

Ironically, even how top judges are selected in some of our countries has increased their power. In fact, the more the rich democratic world moves toward the US constitutional model with its *über*-powerful top judges, the better and better the American system for appointing those judges looks. If we are to have this gainsaying, second-guessing power in the hands of committees of ex-lawyers, let's also be honest about the power they wield and make their appointments process a transparently political one – one with the possibility of nominees being blocked on what amounts to party political grounds, say due to their views on how the constitution ought to be interpreted.

Those of us in the Commonwealth world might even want to abandon our practise of calling the reasons judges give for their decisions "judgments" and move over to calling them what Americans do, namely "opinions." On fundamental moral and political line-drawing issues this seems to me a far more apt term. It is part and parcel of my general belief that the more inflated a country allows the moral and political powers of judges to become, the better and better the US system looks.

For majoritarians like me that is very much a backhanded compliment, by the way, though compliment it most certainly is.

INTERNATIONAL LAW

We turn now to international law, the next major cause of democratic decline in our five countries. In fact the more one looks at how international law is created, and who makes it, the less democratic its credentials appear. Even its overall quality is lousy – lousy when compared to law that emerges from the democratic structures in the United States, the UK, Canada, Australia, or New Zealand. It no doubt isn't lousy compared to the law in place in undemocratic countries such as Sudan, North Korea, Libya, Syria, and China, or even pseudo-democratic ones such as Venezuela, Russia, and Pakistan. But as the British comedian John Cleese was wont to say, his tone dripping sarcasm, "that's high praise indeed." Our focus is on five of the oldest democracies on the planet, and compared to their domestic law the quality of international law really is substandard, the way it is made is horribly lacking in transparency, and democratic legitimacy and accountability are virtually wholly absent.

Over two centuries ago the philosopher, prison reformer, advocate of ever greater democracy and legal commentator Jeremy Bentham – famous today still for his exposition of the doctrine of utilitarianism[29] – attacked the common law.[30] Bentham thought there were big problems with this sort of judge-made law that we in Australia, New Zealand, the United States, the UK, and Canada all call "the common law." First off, it was retrospective. Judges made it at the point of application at the end of a lawsuit focused on things that had already happened so that any changes in doctrine, however they might be dressed up, effectively had altered the rules of the game for the side that had relied on how things stood before this change of doctrine (say, for an anachronistic instance, the duties owed by a manufacturer to consumers of those goods not in a contractual relationship with that manufacturer). The contrast with statute law enacted by an elected legislature and set to come into force on some specified future date could not be any more stark as regards this issue of the retrospectivity of the common law.

The next problem Bentham identified was related to that first one. You see, in order to mask that retrospective element many supporters of the common law talked as though the real, true common law had always been out there in the ether. For them, any change in doctrine announced by the judges amounted to telling the rest of us what had always been the correct understanding of the law. It just hadn't been properly understood as such until now.

Think of this as the "one right answer" or "judges just discovering what was always out there" or "it was implicitly part of the best understanding of the settled case law, though earlier judges hadn't yet recognized it" view of the common law. It solved the problem of retrospectivity. But the cure was in various respects worse than the disease. It was worse because it rested on a patent and palpable fiction, that judges weren't ever making law at the point of application. No, they were merely announcing what had always been the law or the best understanding of earlier case law. Bentham had a field day with such claims which rely on pretending that judge-made law, the common law, does not involve any discretionary input by the judges who definitively decide a case. So this was another ground he had for disparaging the common law.

Bentham also thought it was too unsystematic and unfocused on achieving the greatest happiness of the greatest number, this common law. But he also saw this sort of judge-made law as supremely undemocratic. Those who extolled the common law at least had to concede, thought Bentham, that it was the product of an unrepresentative, unaccountable lawyerly caste – "Judge & Co." – whose views and interests and values often could and sometimes did differ from those of the majority. In such circumstances why should the judges' views become law? On what grounds was that legitimate?

These last three paragraphs on Jeremy Bentham might seem to be something of a digression (at best) or irrelevancy (at worst). They're not. I put them in because one of the things I want to claim in this section is that international law is desperately in need of its own Jeremy Bentham, someone who ruthlessly debunks its pretensions and shortfalls and illegitimacies.

In this book we will only be scratching the surface, and limiting ourselves to the undemocratic aspects of international law (or rather, to be fair, some parts of international law). Having said that, a strong case can be made for thinking international law, or the parts of it I will be concentrating on, is worse than the common law when it comes to its undemocratic effects. Far worse, in fact. Everyone accepted that a statute overruled and trumped the judge-made common law when the two were inconsistent. By no means at all does everyone accept that international law must lose to inconsistent domestic statute law. Some even think the international variety ought to trump a country's highest constitutional law. So the flaws and weaknesses and inefficiencies and opacities and illegitimacies of the former cry out even more for detailing and debunking. As I said, we will only be scratching the surface of that task.

Case Study

How many readers have found themselves unable to sleep on some night and so decided to read the 1989 United Nations Convention on the Rights of the Child (CRC)? Implausible, I know, even for lawyers, but it's not the worst strategy for overcoming insomnia. And in your late night browsing you would come across article 19 of that convention or treaty.

It reads in part as follows: "State Parties shall take all appropriate legislative, administrative, social and educational measures to protect the child from all forms of physical or mental violence." Now think about what you figure that covers and doesn't cover. And remember that all these multilateral treaties like the CRC have to be worded so as to get on board as many as possible of the world's Sudans, Chinas, Libyas, and presumably worse – and I say worse because in 2010 Muammar Gaddafi's Libya was overwhelmingly voted on to the UN Human Rights Council, to be there along with a bunch of other countries from which no sane person in any of the five democratic nations we're concerned with in this book would take human rights advice. (Libya stayed there until its bombings of its own citizens in 2011 eventually saw it removed.)

However, the failings of the UN Human Rights Council and its predecessor the Commission on Human Rights, not least the way authoritarian regimes manage to get voted on to these bodies and the patently unbalanced obsession they have with Israel, are well known. My point here is something else, namely that it's not at all clear what that article 19 of the CRC means. Yes, we know that a lot of countries whose standards look pretty awful compared to those in our five countries signed up to the CRC. And we know that almost all countries at the time of signing of the CRC permitted parents to spank or smack their own children, if the degree of force was reasonable.

Now let's say some democratic government, say one like Australia or Canada or New Zealand or the UK or the United States, had a statute (at the national or state level) that allowed parents to spank their kids. Would you say that that statute allowing corporal punishment breached human rights? Let me put that question slightly differently. Would your decision on whether parental corporal punishment infringed human rights depend upon the proper interpretation of article 19 of the CRC or even be influenced in the least by article 19? And if you thought parental spanking did *not* breach human rights, but you learned some overseas experts (or, rather, self-styled experts) thought otherwise – ones who were wholly undemocratically chosen and included people from countries that were undemocratic and even from downright authoritarian regimes – would you defer to them? Would it matter to you in the least what this handful of self-styled experts thought?

These are not off-the-wall questions. This is not a pointless hypothetical. You see all the big United Nations conventions or multilateral treaties, including the CRC, have committees that are set up to monitor the progress in implementing the conventions of all the states that have signed up to them.

Now at this point you might like to know a couple of key things. First, the membership of all these monitoring committees is determined in a less than transparent way – nothing remotely close to how US Supreme Court justices are picked – that comes nowhere near letting anyone claim those selected have been democratically appointed, or anointed. Second, committee membership includes, indeed it is weighted toward, those from countries you wouldn't take any moral advice from if your life depended on it.

Third, and this is the point to take on board if you only remember one, the Committee for the CRC has consistently maintained that parental corporal punishment violates the CRC convention.

When you learned that fact, and fact it is, would your view of the acceptability of parental spanking change? Let's assume it would not. (It certainly would make no difference to me.) What if I told you, in rather more grandiose terms, that international law required that you not spank your kids because such spanking was a breach of their human rights as set out in article 19 of the CRC? (After all, this is what the CRC Committee thinks.[31])

Two roads now diverge. Go down one of them and you simply outsource your view of the acceptability of spanking to the Committee for the CRC. You defer to this handful of self-styled experts, perhaps in the name of complying with international law, or because you think the Committee is best placed to know what the vague, amorphous article 19 provisions mean, or even due to your desire to be part of a chardonnay-sipping metropolitan elite in your home country. Whatever the reason for deferring to the Committee, and its view of the reach, aegis and ambit of article 19, this is one option. Spanking breaches human rights, this I know because international law and the Committee tell me so.

Go down the other road, however, and you refuse to be swayed by what this UN Committee set-up to monitor the CRC thinks. This refusal, in its turn, can be motivated by two different concerns. In other words, not very far down this second road you find it splits or bifurcates. You find one path focuses on international law itself, accepts its core level legitimacy in resolving such issues as parental corporal punishment, but makes legalistic arguments for why the Committee is wrong in its understanding of article 19. These legalistic rejoinders would no doubt focus on the legislative history of the CRC – what the states that signed up to it intended it to cover, your claim being that they did not intend it to cover parental spanking. To buttress this claim about the intentions of the state parties who signed it you would probably point to the fact that at the time of signing virtually all the countries signing up to the CRC had domestic legal systems that allowed spanking. This would be external evidence of likely intentions, it being unlikely that a government of a country with spanking would knowingly sign up to a treaty forbidding spanking. And even if one or two governments did, perhaps to sidestep the need to change domestic law, it is implausible in the extreme that almost all governments signing up to the CRC did this. Certainly it is unlikely in the extreme most democratic governments did.

Notice that those who travel down this sub-branch of the second road do *not* make core level objections to international law itself being relevant, if not determinative. No, they effectively simply argue for a different understanding of the proper meaning of article 19. Where the Committee of the CRC seems to see it as a metaphorical living tree, whose reach and meaning are not determined by the intentions of those state parties that signed it, those travelling down this sub-branch want it interpreted differently, perhaps according to some form of originalism or other. They don't shun or reject or belittle international law itself. Some may seek a halfway house and say international law or the views of the Committee are not determinative and conclusive, merely a guide that is relevant and needs to be considered. Meanwhile some may reject the Committee and its views in favour of the text itself, a sort of Protestant approach to what international law does and doesn't demand.

Of course this second road of refusing to be swayed by what the CRC Committee thinks about spanking has another, different sub-branch. Travellers down this one do not make legalistic arguments about how the Committee has erred in its understanding of what article 19 covers. No, much more fundamentally they simply do not accept the core level applicability of international law to the question of whether parents in some of the oldest democracies in the world can or cannot spank their children. They not only dismiss the views of this handful of UN-appointed Committee members; they dismiss, too, the relevance of international law itself to the issue. For many such travellers down this second sub-branch of this second road, it will be the fundamental lack of democratic legitimacy when it comes to international law that motivates their position.

I am much of their mind. If issues such as parental spanking are covered, in whole or in part, by an international law treaty couched in indeterminate, abstract terms, then it must follow that the scope for democratic decision-making and letting-the-numbers-count majoritarianism has been narrowed and enervated.

As it happens, though not purely by chance, this example of the CRC and spanking can show us two ways in which international law of the treaty-based kind is democratically deficient. Once we've seen both those, we can move on to a much worse sort of international law – worse in the countermajoritarian, anti-democratic sense that is. But put that other sort of international law out of your mind till I get to it shortly and focus for now on the sort that flows from countries, nation-states, signing up to treaties and conventions.

Start with Canada, Australia, New Zealand, and the United Kingdom. All four have ratified or signed up to the CRC. As I said earlier in this book, doing so in a Westminster system is easier than in the United States. The executive can do so without any veto or block lying in the hands of any part of the legislature (though there are half-hearted nods toward Parliament in the UK, as I have mentioned). As I put it above, ratified treaties or conventions have less democratic legitimacy in Australia, the UK, Canada, and New Zealand than they do in the United States. This point is often overlooked. And for all of us majoritarian democrats it is America that looks better in this comparison.

Now if you go back forty or fifty years, there was a trade-off outside the United States for this lack of legislative input when it came to treaties and conventions. That trade-off was simply this: The executive could ratify and sign up to treaties all by itself, yes. But such treaties did *not*, let me doubly stress that negative, become part of the country's domestic law. It applied, perhaps, internationally. It did not apply domestically – not unless it was incorporated into the country's internal laws by also being passed as a statute by the elected legislature.

In the absence of a ratified treaty being explicitly incorporated into domestic law in this way, it was not a source of valid law. You couldn't argue in court that you should win because of this treaty; you couldn't argue that the written constitution meant this, rather than that, because of this treaty; you couldn't even argue that a statute meant X rather than Y because of this treaty.

In that now bygone world, the American approach to treaties and conventions was in fact *not* more democratic than the approach in the Westminster world. Sure, the Americans took treaties more seriously back then and one might have made an argument for the US approach on that basis, that we shouldn't ratify a treaty unless we are prepared to make it enforceable law. That sort of argument would cash out in rule of law terms, or "don't deal in aspirations" terms. But in no sense was the old Westminster approach to treaties any less democratic than the US approach. Americans did, and do, take treaties very seriously indeed and demand that they pass through the elected upper house Senate on a supermajoritarian basis. Our Westminster countries did not, and do not, demand this but then a half-century ago the executive ratified treaties did not become part of the domestic law. Your average voter could ignore them. Full stop.

That is no longer the case in our Westminster countries. Judges have changed that. Administrative law, the rules and regulations below the level of statute law and including judge-made ones about how tribunals must operate and who must be heard, became permeated with rules plucked by judges from these treaties. Then statutes started to be interpreted with reference to these treaties from international law. It did not matter that the treaties were *not* in orthodox terms part of the domestic law in Westminster systems. The lack of democratic legitimacy compared to a US-type set-up for ratifying treaties didn't matter to the judges either.

You know the game. First you start by appealing to treaties (however vague, amorphous, indeterminate or couched in moral abstractions – "all appropriate ... measures to protect the child from ... violence") when the statute is ambiguous, and only then. That seems fairly harmless. So after a while, once that has bedded down, you go further. You make what the treaties say the presumptive way of interpreting all statutes, so that only explicit, clear words in the statute overcome that presumption. No reason is given for why this should be the default position or why an unincorporated treaty with patently flawed democratic credentials should have such power to influence the meaning of the legislature's statutes, some enacted before the treaty was even signed and ratified. You just move on as though it's self-evident that democratically enacted statutes ought to be interpreted through the prism of this sort of treaty and convention focused international law.

From there it's a moderately short step to using these unincorporated treaties as filters for interpreting the written constitution. That's what happens in Canada, though Australia still holds out against that last step, barely.[32] Meanwhile in the UK and New Zealand there are no written constitutions, which forecloses this final step of using unincorporated treaties as filters for the task of constitutional interpretation. Alas, that only means that using them to help decide what statutes mean in the UK and New Zealand is even more problematic and potentially countermajoritarian. There, statutes matter more. So interpreting them through the prism of treaties matters more too.

I said above there are two ways in which international law of the treaty-based kind is democratically deficient. And I've now outlined the first way. It happens in our four Westminster countries when treaties *that have been signed and ratified* are used by the judges to help make and re-make administrative law and also to aid in interpreting statutes and constitutional provisions even to the point of making these treaties the default, presumptive positions of what statutes mean. And all this even though these treaties and conventions have not been incorporated into domestic law and are not – on the orthodox understanding that takes democratic concerns seriously – part of the domestic law. That's the first way, and it applies only to our four Westminster countries.

The second way is worse. And this second way happens most publicly and most notoriously in the United States, possibly because of the very fact that Americans take ratifying treaties very seriously indeed and expect them to win clear democratic support at least in the Senate.

What happens on this second scenario, and it's not easily defended if you are a democrat, is this: Judges once again are interpreting domestic legal texts like statutes and constitutional provisions, just as above. And again the judges are doing this interpreting by referring to treaties or conventions – they may be looking to the treaties for evidence of international views on some issue or for a moral consensus on some rights-based disagreement or to see what meaning to give some morally charged phrase or term or something else. For our purposes, that is beside the point when it comes to this second way in which treaty-based international law is democratically wanting, deficient, and exiguous. What is the point is that on this second scenario the treaties and conventions the judges use *have not even been ratified*. They have failed to win a majority vote in the Senate, if we focus on the United States for a moment. These are therefore unratified treaties without the imprimatur or approval of the domestic democratic politics. Either the treaty failed to win Senate approval or it was not even put to the Senate or the president himself did not sign up to it.

And yet the judges use such a treaty to help them interpret, say, the US Constitution.

Farfetched? No. For instance, this is precisely what happened back in 2005 in *Roper v. Simmons*.[33] The US Supreme Court in that case cited the CRC in the course of deciding what no "cruel and unusual punishments" meant in the Eighth Amendment. The issue for those judges was whether the US Bill of Rights meant they could strike down or invalidate democratically enacted laws that allowed for the possibility of executing juveniles?

In deciding that question a majority of US Supreme Court justices, as I said, cited the CRC, the very same Convention on the Rights of the Child we've been using throughout this case-study section. But here's the thing. The United States has never ratified this CRC. It has no democratic standing or pedigree at all. None. Zero. And yet it is being used to tell us what the two-centuries-old US Bill of Rights, and its Eighth Amendment, mean.

It doesn't stop there. In that same case the judges (or those in the majority) cited another treaty. This was the International Covenant on Civil and Political Rights (ICCPR). This treaty had been ratified by the United States, or rather most of it had. Not all of it though. The United States had entered a formal reservation against the ICCPR's no-death-penalty provision, meaning that part of the treaty didn't apply in the United States. But the judges in *Roper* cited it anyway in the context of a death-penalty case.

Let me be blunt. Top American judges in the course of deciding whether they would gainsay and overrule democratically elected legislators by invalidating one of their statutes decided to cite and give weight to treaties that the elected political branches had rejected; they cited and gave weight to treaty-based international law that the elected branches had specifically and explicitly refused to incorporate into domestic law. These top US judges – and it is only fair to say it wasn't all of them – exercised their countermajoritarian, anti-democratic Bill of Rights power to strike down statutes, but not before referring to, considering, citing, and presumably putting at least some weight on an international treaty the democratically accountable branches had flat out rejected. Wow! This is *not* letting the numbers count, times two. It's anti-democratic juristocracy or kritarchy or international law genuflecting on stilts.

Now supporters of this sort of use of non-ratified treaty-based international law will point out that the top US judges who did this said they decided based on domestic materials and only mentioned or cited the CRC and ICCPR as "confirmation" of what they had anyway decided – namely, to invalidate a democratically enacted law. Some supporters might even try to make a more subtle, some might say sophistical, point. They might suggest that these majority judges were using these non-ratified treaties as evidence of a consensus of the practice of other states, not as part of an attempt to discern some norm of international law. (Take it from me, the former is supposedly less objectionable than the latter.)

However those attempts, and others, to explain away and legitimate this second way of using treaty-based international law will not satisfy the majoritarian democrat. Not by a long shot. Such attempts fall laughably short of providing a persuasive defence for top American judges doing this.

Yet some past and present US Supreme Court justices vigorously defend this, and reliance on international law more generally, when speaking extra-judicially (meaning outside their day job of deciding cases that reach the Supreme Court, say when writing a law review article or giving a speech). Take just a few examples. Justice Stephen Breyer is a committed advocate of using international law in this way (and indeed was one of those in the majority in *Roper* who did so). Justice Ruth Ginsburg can be described in similar terms, and was on the same majority side in *Roper*. In 2005, when giving the keynote address to the Ninety-Ninth Annual Meeting of the American Society of International Law, Ginsburg was vigorous in her defence of citing, referring to, and appealing to international law.[34] She saw that as one of the "common denominators of basic fairness between the governors and the governed." Even Republican-appointed former Justice Sandra Day O'Connor, giving the keynote address to the same society three years earlier, said that "conclusions reached by ... the international community should at times constitute persuasive authority in American courts."[35]

The goal of this case study has been to make the reader doubt assertions such as those from Sandra Day O'Connor and Ruth Ginsburg (to say nothing of whole boatloads of law journal articles by legal academics that are even more gung-ho about using treaty-based international law to influence how the US Constitution is interpreted).

Take the debate down from the Olympian heights of disagreement-finessing abstractions to the quagmire of drawing highly contestable social policy lines – ones having to do with whether parents can spank their children for instance – and it is not at all clear to me why treaty-based international law should influence in any way at all how the US Bill of Rights is interpreted; and it is out-and-out democratically illegitimate to pay any heed to a non-ratified treaty like the CRC.

So the authoritative scope for deciding issues by letting the numbers count goes down – it reduces or declines or becomes smaller – when judges appeal to non-ratified treaties in the United States to influence in any way how they interpret important legal texts. The same is true when judges in our four Westminster countries appeal to any treaties at all, even ratified ones, to give meaning to their important legal texts, leaving to one side instances where a treaty is put into the form of a statute and incorporated into domestic law by being passed by the legislature.

This all means that the majoritarian democrat can complain that the field that was formerly left for resolving issues by the elected branches has been narrowed and shrunk by this appeal to treaty-based international law. This complaint does not require that the fields in all five of our countries started at the same size – we saw in part I of this book that the starting points were all different. Nor does the grievance depend upon the same inroads being made into democracy in all five countries by this treaty-based international law. That too differs.

It is the fact of *any* decline or shrinking that concerns and angers the partisan of democracy. This case study has shown one way one sort of international law, the treaty-based sort, can cause that decline. It does not matter whether you, the reader, agree with some group of UN bureaucrats or committee members on the CRC that spanking is wrong, or even that spanking infringes rights. We are not debating substantive moral positions here. We are asking how such positions ought to be determined in a world where well-informed, nice, reasonable, smart people disagree about the moral rights and wrongs of spanking. As Jeremy Waldron puts it, we are asking about how best or most legitimately to resolve reasonable disagreements in society.[36] Do we count everyone as equal and vote to elect representatives who will decide – knowing in advance that all of us will sometimes be on the winning side of democratic decision-making and sometimes on the losing side? Or do we put that aside when it comes to issues such as spanking or the death penalty and let treaty-based international law play a role in deciding what to do?

If you opt to go down the latter route, you are part of a very recent trend, at most decades old. Here is how the late Lord Rodger, then of the UK's new Supreme Court (formerly known as the Judicial Committee of the House of Lords and still its top court) describes this trend:

> My impression is that much of the writing on public international law to which we are referred is slanted towards a particular result that the writer wishes to see prevail as the law. It often appears that the writers have, say, a particular human rights agenda and that their book or article is written with a view to securing that it will come to form part of the corpus of writings which help to shape the law. Indeed, often the writers sit on some international tribunal or other body which deals with the same matter. On occasions, however, it is difficult to see how the writer's argument is to be squared with the wording of the particular international instrument in question – however desirable the result may be.[37]

So this is another trend that infringes on the scope for democratic decision-making. This appeal to treaty-based international law (in its various guises and levels of toxicity) is another cause of today's decline in democracy, of taking these decisions, in whole or in part, out of the hands of voters.

Believe it or not things get worse from here.

Non-treaty-Based (or Undressed) International Law

So far we have been considering only one sort of international law. It's the sort most readers will be aware of and will think of when someone mentions or refers to international law. This is the treaty-based sort. Countries get together and agree to a treaty or convention. Perhaps it's a General Agreement on Tariffs and Trade (GATT) or it's a CRC or an ICCPR. Not all countries sign up to them. Not all countries ratify them. Some that do are democratic countries; others that do are not – indeed some countries that sign up are out-and-out authoritarian regimes.

Among the democratic ones, the process for entering into and ratifying these treaties will vary. Yet in all of them it will involve some step that confers at least some democratic legitimacy. After all, even in Westminster systems such as those in Canada, the UK, Australia, and New Zealand the executive is part of the elected branches. It has democratic legitimacy and accountability. Of course the democratic respectability of treaties in those jurisdictions is less than it is in the United States, noticeably less in fact. But it's not zero or non-existent.

Remember that because the next sort of international law we will look at literally has no democratic input or warrant or genealogy or respectability at all. None. It is even worse than where top judges use non-ratified treaties to help guide how they interpret their own country's constitution, if that is conceivable.

I am going to call this other sort of international law, the sort that does *not* flow from treaties or conventions, "undressed international law." I call it that because it hasn't yet been dressed-up or formalized into a treaty. It hasn't yet been agreed to by any democratically elected and accountable legislators or members of the executive branch. To the extent it limits what any of our five democratic countries can do, it is a cause of democratic decline precisely in the sense this book set out to bemoan, lament and reverse.

This undressed international law is known in legal academic circles as customary international law. Its content cannot be found by looking in some treaty or convention, whether one's country has signed up to and ratified that treaty or not. No, this undressed international law which we turn to now is the law that is inferred from the practice of States (or countries). Once a consistent and general practice of states has been identified – and note that this general state practice has to be something that was followed out of a sense of legal obligation – then it becomes part of this undressed international law and its binding legal norms. International custom just is that which has been identified as widespread state practice (when it has been engaged in out of a sense of legal obligation).

Now throughout that last paragraph I deliberately used the passive voice. I spoke of practices that "are inferred" and "have been identified" so as intentionally to mask or gloss over the rather important question of who gets to do all this inferring and identifying and deciding just when it is – and is not – that states are following some practice or other, and following it out of a sense of legal obligation.

The beauty of the passive voice is that it can give the subtle impression that these practices somehow identify themselves, or that some omniscient and unerring God is doing the identifying and inferring and exercising of otherwise fallible judgment. It can help remove from centre stage the fundamental issue of *who* precisely it is that makes these inferences and identifies these practices and decides not just that a practice exists, but that it is motivated by a sense of legal obligation.

In a book such as this about democracy and democratic control over the content of law that simply will not do. So let us put away this dissembling and finessing use of the passive voice, which I confess I indulged in to illustrate one way the issue of democratic input into the content of undressed international law can be downplayed. Let us put away this intentionally temporary and short-lived use of the passive voice then and start by focusing explicitly on these "who makes it" and "where's the democratic input?" questions.

Start with the former query. The unadorned answer is that what are termed "publicists" determine this undressed international law. The Statute of the International Court of Justice says it is "the most highly qualified publicists" who have the role of determining this subsidiary sort of international law.

Many of those falling into the category of "publicists" are legal academics; they are law professors. Not all law professors of course. You have to be someone who is knowledgeable and writes in this field of international law. So you have to show technical mastery in the field. But you also have to demonstrate to those already recognized as being highly qualified publicists that you have what Harvard law professor Mark Tushnet describes as "soundness."

> Soundness seems to require that one be committed to the project of international law, that is, to the proposition that nation-states ought to resolve an ever-increasing number and ever-wider range of their disputes pursuant to existing and emergent rules of international law rather than, for example, by economic or, worse, military force.[38]

Let me be a bit blunter. No one gets to vote for these legal academic publicists. They have no democratic warrant at all. Even if we assumed that law professors as a group shared broadly similar political and moral views to the population at large – and that assumption is plain out false and ridiculous, in the US international law professors from elite universities contribute to the Democrats over the Republicans by a ratio of well over five to one[39] – this would still be immensely unrepresentative because only those unskeptical about the benefits of an ever-increasing role and scope for undressed (and dressed) international law can ever make it into the club.

With a rather enjoyable dollop of understatement, Mark Tushnet goes on to comment on this "soundness" criterion, this need to be committed to the project, before an otherwise technically proficient law professor can qualify as a publicist. Tushnet puts it rather drily as follows: "This feature of the process of becoming a publicist gives the academic field some degree of self-containment. One is writing in part for other legal academics, to achieve and sustain one's position as a publicist. But only in part, because one is also writing for others committed to the project of international law, including notably decision-makers in institutions that clearly do make international law, such as judges on international tribunals and members of the International Law Commission."[40]

In terms of who makes this undressed or customary international law we have not yet moved beyond the part of publicists made up of law professors and already there are rather massive deficiencies in terms of democratic input. First off, law professors as a whole are significantly (to put it mildly) to the left of voters at large in their political and moral views. Second, it is not all knowledgeable, technically accomplished international law legal academics who get to be publicists, and so get to identify these practices of nation-states. It is only that portion of the law professors who are considered "sound" when it comes to their commitment to the international law project. Think of a self-selecting lawyerly caste of committed experts, and you'll get the general idea.

It is not difficult in the least to point out that excluding those who have a modicum of skepticism about international law's benefits is an undemocratic roadblock or filter. We supporters of a thin, unvarnished sort of majoritarian, letting-the-numbers-count democracy start with the core premise that you count everyone equally then count heads. There are no "We don't like your views or values" exclusions or filters at this initial stage. Yet that sort of exclusion or filter is precisely what there is when it comes to who qualifies as a law professor publicist.

That makes this sort of law doubly deficient in democratic terms. Law professors as a whole are nowhere near being representative of voters; they are vastly more left-wing, on average, across the board, at least in the cosmopolitan left-wing lawyers sense, if not the union left-wing sense. And even among international law professors as a whole, only true believers in the international law project have any realistic prospect of becoming a publicist – someone who gets to infer and identify what the supposed duty-motivated practices of states are, and so tell us the content of this undressed international law.

This isn't letting-the-numbers-count law-making. It's more like law-making by a caste of experts with views known to diverge from those of the majority, or rather by those from that caste who can in addition pass a test of ideological purity.

When issues come up such as over the death penalty, or whether what is known as hate speech must be criminalized, or how to structure labour laws, why should the laws on these issues that have been decided by the elected representatives of the voters lose out to, or even be influenced in any way by customary international law, by this thoroughly undemocratic (and doubly so) undressed international law?

One of the trends of the recent past is that customary international law, or undressed international law, has expanded its reach. It never used to concern itself with a nation's treatment of its own citizens. It very much was about the "law of nations." Restricted in that way, as it used to be, one might still balk and say that a democracy such as the United States or the UK is better placed to decide on the advisability of, say, pre-emptive war, better than some insular caste of publicists rummaging through the entrails of supposedly perceived state practices. However, go back before undressed international law expanded its reach into the realm of how a nation-state treated its own citizens, and you can see that its scope for conflict with majoritarian, letting-the-numbers-count, democratic law-making is pretty small.

Perhaps I can make that point in a better way. If some journalist or non-governmental organization (NGO) or law professor is going to accuse an elected government of violating international law (of the undressed variety), the scope and ambit for doing so is considerably, considerably smaller where that same undressed international law confines itself to matters between nations. You might find a few accusations about the illegality of pre-emptive war (though no doubt made in the context of Iraq rather than Kosova), but not much in addition to that.

However, allow undressed international law to inflate and to expand its supposed jurisdiction to include how a nation treats its own citizens, and the scope for conflict with the rules made by democratically elected lawmakers multiplies exponentially – making suddenly relevant domestic laws on hate speech, or workplace relations, or the death penalty, or anything in fact that can be translated or transliterated into the language of human rights.

Of course that comparative assessment – that domestic law looks better in terms of quality, effectiveness and legitimacy than international law – is only true of democracies. As regards most non-democracies, and certainly military juntas, theocracies, and one-party states, international law looks better than domestic law when it comes to how a nation treats its own citizens. In other words, there's an asymmetry at work, even as regards legitimacy. The wilder exponents of cultural relativism may wish to dissemble at this point, or brazenly to claim that international law is better than the domestic law of both non-democracies and democracies.

That sort of "international law is better" response fails both for being untrue and also for being somewhat (or wholly) inconsistent. It's untrue because as a plain matter of empirical fact democracies produce superior domestic laws to non-democracies (pretty much across the board but especially when it comes to the sort of individual liberty and freedom entitlements that lie at the heart of those matters labelled "human rights concerns"). And they are not just a little bit superior. They are massively so. And these domestic laws of democracies are superior to international law as well, not just because the treaty-based sort requires compromises to get non-democracies on board but because the undressed sort is made by such an unrepresentative and unaccountable cohort.

One might be tempted, I suppose, to pretend that undressed international law is superior to all versions of domestic law, whether it come from non-democracies or democracies, and indulge in this pretense simply as a ruse to allow international law's precepts to prevail in non-democracies, where they would clearly be an improvement. This would amount to the "little white lie" school of thinking. It would run something as follows: "I will assert the superiority and jurisdictional dominance of undressed international law over all types of domestic law, not because it's true, but simply because I calculate that that fiction or sleight of hand will have the best chance of extending the norms of undressed international law in the world's non-democracies. And the benefits of that would outweigh the costs and negatives and downsides of having them leech into the world's democracies."

One might be tempted by that line of thinking, but it is a temptation to be resisted. Here's its fatal flaw or conceit. The world's nasty regimes will ignore undressed international law (and no doubt the treaty-based sort too) when it comes to how they treat their own citizens, and they will ignore it regardless of how far these international law norms influence and reshape things in the world's democracies. That's the irony. If your unspoken goal is to reform non-democracies for the better by proclaiming the superiority and pre-eminence of undressed (and no doubt dressed) international law, you will find that that doesn't come to pass. Instead, you will end up influencing only the democracies, and on balance for the worse. Therein lies the irony or flaw in this "little white lie" way of thinking.

So in my view any assertions along the lines that international law is better than the domestic law of democracies is untrue, and doubly so when we factor in the legitimacy benefits of "rule by the people" as opposed to "rule by international law publicists." That said, such assertions about the supposed superiority of undressed international law are also inconsistent in a way. At least that's the case if the first step or prong in the argument involves an unwillingness to say that the domestic laws of democracies (on average, over time, and overwhelmingly) are markedly superior to and better than those of non-democracies. Let's suppose one subscribes to a version of cultural relativism that forecloses judging between the laws of democracies and non-democracies – "Who am I to judge?" "Isn't this just my culturally inculcated view, your differently inculcated view not being measurable against or comparable to mine?" Take your pick of this sort of flabby, insipid, and unconvincing line of thought.

My point is that if you feel you can't judge between the domestic law of democracies and non-democracies (weighing them up in terms of their competing effectiveness, legitimacy and overall consequences), then you surely must also be foreclosed from asserting that undressed international law is better than or superior to any sort of domestic law, whatever its provenance. Thinking yourself not in a position to be able to judge any X better than Y is not a worldview that you can turn on and off at will, or when convenient, or when it suits your core level political preferences.

Thus far we have only considered one group of contributors to undressed international law, those international law professors who not only have sufficient technical expertise but who also have been adjudged thoroughly sound and committed to its ongoing and expanding reach and influence. True, it is not at all clear or definite who it is that dispenses the "you are sound" label or guarantee. True, this group is in no way at all democratically chosen, or accountable, or representative; indeed, as a group it is self-selecting or self-appointed. These publicists may have virtues when it comes to their role as lawmakers, but none of those virtues has any connection at all to democracy.

We can see this in plain terms from one unashamed (and in no way unique) supporter who tells us flat out that nation-states do not make customary or undressed international law, no it is made by the "people that care; the professors, the writers of textbooks and case books, and the authors of articles in leading international law journals."[41]

That being so, and this being the highly unrepresentative and non-majoritarian group that it is, it follows that as undressed international law expands its reach and scope and authority in the democratic world the result is at least some lessening or contraction of the scope, reach and authority of majoritarian, democratic decision-making. We may still count everyone as equal and let the numbers count, but they will count for less than they did before this expansion of undressed international law. Democracy, if only in small part and at the margins, will have declined.

The picture for majoritarian democrats does not improve when we turn to the other main group of people who make undressed international law. These are the judges, the international law judges.

Here we need to consider the United Nations' International Court of Justice (ICJ). Fifteen justices or judges sit on this court. Depending on how you categorize Venezuela and Russia, between a third and a half of the ICJ judges come from non-democracies (which is a more circumspect and polite way of indicating that they hail as well from repressive, authoritarian regimes such as Sierra Leone, China, and Morocco). And given how they are selected, they lack even the indirect democratic credentials of top judges in most of our five countries who are appointed by the elected branches (Canada, New Zealand, Australia, and the United States) and then subject to a transparent and sometimes unsuccessful confirmation hearing (the United States).

To become an ICJ judge, by contrast, a candidate needs to be approved by both a majority of General Assembly countries and a majority of Security Council countries. As you would expect this is a process chock full of lobbying and glad-handling and vote-trading and buying among regional blocs and other sorts of groupings. In that sense it is a highly politicized process, indeed one where luck and fortuitous timing play a big role. Having conceded that, you can see that the appointments process for ICJ judges is nothing like the US system for appointing and confirming Supreme Court justices. Both are politicized, but in different ways. The US system forces candidates to answer highly charged questions. Those questions can be evaded, for sure, but they nevertheless get to be asked in a very public way. As well, the nominee's personal outlook and sensibilities can be raised. And most noticeably, candidates once nominated are sometimes rejected and blocked. In other words, there is a form of public deliberation, albeit an attenuated one.

The ICJ appointments procedure is opaque to the nth degree in comparison. It is backroom, horse-trading, factional politics, where geography is a big factor.[42] More to our point, it involves politics devoid of democratic concerns or overtones. Even within democratic countries the nominating of an ICJ candidate is insulated from any direct governmental input – an insulation that may be desirable when it comes to authoritarian regimes (though I suspect such regimes have more tools for getting their preferred candidate nominated anyway), but not for democratic ones.

Take the United States. The president does not nominate American candidates for ICJ openings. Instead, nominations are made by something called a "national group" at the Permanent Court of Arbitration at The Hague. It is the members of these "national groups" that are nominated by national governments. In a democracy, where a government's recourse in the face of an unwanted nomination is highly constrained, these groups are insulated from public accountability and control by the elected government. In non-democracies, as I suggested above, governments probably have tools for getting their national group people to give them the nominee they want, tools that are unavailable – and unwanted – in a democracy.

On top of all that, the ICJ is not well known to citizens of democratic countries, or indeed to those of non-democratic nations. The percentage of Americans that could name even a single ICJ judge, whether American or otherwise, would be vanishingly small. The same goes for citizens of Australia, Canada, and the United Kingdom. New Zealand might possibly do marginally better on this count because their first ever ICJ nominee, Professor Ken Keith, made it successfully on to the court in the relatively recent past. But the self-congratulatory press for that milestone has long since ebbed away, so it is probably much the same in New Zealand as elsewhere. The ICJ gets little press; it is poorly understood; its judges are unknown, even in legal circles (if we except those working in the field of international law).

To sum up, then, the democratic credentials of the international law judges, those on the International Court of Justice, are slight to non-existent. They lack even the indirect democratic credentials of judges in democracies, at least where judges are appointed by the elected branches and not by judicial appointments commissions (as in the UK).

It gets worse of course, because there is also the issue of the reach of undressed customary international law, and whether that is quietly expanding unknown to most citizens in our five long-standing democracies. Of course it may well be that judges on all courts have some interest in increasing the jurisdiction of the court on which they serve. They will be subject to a temptation to increase that jurisdiction, to widen the numbers and sorts of cases their court can hear. Some judges resist this jurisdiction-expanding temptation better than others, but all are subject to it. And this will certainly be so when jurisdiction expands to encompass how a nation treats its own citizens. Yet it will also be affected by the extent of discretionary power that these ICJ judges have when it comes to stating how far this undressed international law does, and does not, extend.

Accordingly, if we are asking about the reach of undressed international law, and we are asking this to the judges of the ICJ who have a vested interest or stake in discerning or discovering or asserting a wider (or indeed ever-wider) scope for this sort of customary international law, then we should not be overly surprised when that is the answer we get (on average, over time). These ICJ judges have discretionary power when it comes to stating how far this undressed international law does, and does not, extend. No disinterested observer would consider them wholly impartial, detached or unbiased on the question of the proper reach of international law.

Think of it in these terms, if you like. If you are a betting person then bet on a gradual ratchet-up effect as far as what the ICJ judges will tell us is the ambit and reach of undressed (and dressed) international law. That bet is as safe as the one the casinos make in Las Vegas.

And when it pays off, or comes true, then in small, even miniscule ways, the corresponding scope for democratic decision-making declines. When that jurisdiction expands to encompass how a nation treats its own citizens, the decline for democracy can be more than small.

As I mentioned above, that has been one of the recent trends, that undressed international law has moved from a purely "law of nations" jurisdiction to one more inflated with at least some role in governing citizen-state interactions and relations.

US law professors John McGinnis and Ilya Somin attribute some of this ratchet-up effect or trend to a split among two schools who see undressed international law in quite different ways. The older school, what they call the "classicists," "believe that customary international law must be rooted in the widespread consensus of the actual practices of nation-states."[43] The job of publicists, on this view, is to look to see what states actually do. It is a question of fact, even on the ancillary issue of what motivates any state action.

Readers will notice that even on this classicist understanding, there will be disagreement. People disagree about facts all the time. And any particular publicist of classicist leanings might think the content of undressed international law is X while a fellow classical school member might think it is X + A or X–Y + B or anything else. But their disagreement about content will be focused on facts, on what the actual practice of states is and on whether such practices – when widespread – are motivated (as a matter of fact) by a sense of legal obligation.

That will make the content of undressed international law inherently debatable and contentious. But notice how much freer of a sense of moral proselytizing and morally pregnant human rights presuppositions it is compared to today's alternative.

That alternative to this older, classical school is the newer, "modern" school. Professors McGinnis and Somin describe it as follows: "Under a more modern concept of international custom, many scholars embrace a methodology that permits substantial human rights norms to be encompassed within customary international law. They relax the classical standards in several ways that accomplish this. Instead of requiring that nation-states actually engage in a practice, they substitute statements by nation-states that give the norms verbal endorsement. These include resolutions of the General Assembly of the United Nations and multilateral treaties."[44]

How many readers knew that? How many, if asked, would have endorsed this move away from an objective (if contentious and disputable) search for what states do to something less factual and more value-laden that builds in a substantial moral component or human rights input regardless of whether such norms are adhered to in fact, or not – and despite the inherently debatable and disputable (and virtually always disputed) nature of human rights norms once they are brought down from the Olympian heights of moral abstractions and applied to real life issues in the quagmire of day-to-day social policy-making?

This newer, modern school relaxes the need to find actual widespread state practice, or what states really do. It relaxes that factual quest in favour of a more morally pregnant or substantive quest to say what states should do. All that is needed are mere statements of verbal endorsement.

Now it seems abundantly clear to me that this newer, modern approach has far more scope to make inroads into democracy. It takes the second component of "acting out of a sense of legal obligation" and turns it from a question of fact ("Is this why states do X?") into one more morally pregnant ("Is this an instance in which we can infer that states *should* feel obliged to do this based on what they have said?"). This amounts to a move from a question of what *is* the case over to a question that adds to that an *ought* or *should* element, and so delivers more jurisdiction-expanding potential. Then there is the issue of who gets to answer that more morally pregnant query. Why it is the democratically unaccountable and unrepresentative judges and law professors who get to answer it. They decide if it would be reasonable to comply with the rule, not you or me or real-life nation-states.

Unfortunately, this newer, modern school is in the ascendant. And that is bad for democracy; it is a cause of democratic decline; it gives more open-ended discretionary power to publicists (meaning a handful of "sound" international law professors) and to a few international law judges appointed in the most opaque way imaginable.

Given the sorts of issues I mentioned above where this undressed international law can impinge on democratic decision-making, not least hate-speech matters, capital punishment, labour relations, and the whole gamut of issues tied to dealing with suspected terrorists, and we democrats have cause to worry. In fact we have good grounds to see the expanding ambit of international law in its entirety as a second main cause of the decline of democracy.

I will finish this section there. My complaint in this book is on the whole a simple one; it is about the declining and narrowing scope for democratic decision-making over the past few decades in five well-established democracies (and probably all well-established democracies); it is about a downward trend that needs reversing.

A related theme I could explore under this rubric of international law would have to do with the need for democratically elected legislative and executive bodies to exit or de-ratify certain treaties that are now outdated and impose obligations on countries that the vast preponderance of citizens reject. Take the Refugees Conventions entered into not long after the Second World War. The numbers of refugees then were a tiny fraction of the tens of millions today; the problem did not seem an open-ended one; there were fewer opportunities for economic refugees to pass themselves off as political ones, and no well-developed black market forces and players there to help and coach them; no one knew how judges would interpret these treaties; there were no real NGO lobby groups established in recipient countries seeking to maximize the percentage of successful applicants; it was a very different world that produced the treaties that today govern refugee migration.

Yet in a sense what is here lacking in this example is simply democratic and political will. Yes, treaties and conventions (as with all laws) grow old and outdated. But the elected governments in our five countries could do something about that if they chose. So such examples fall outside this part of the book and its focus on the causes of democratic decline. In a tangential way I will return to this point later in this book.

SUPRANATIONAL ORGANIZATIONS

Judges and their expansive, often externally unconstrained approaches to interpreting key legal texts were the first cause of democratic decline we looked at above. The second was international law, both as regards its treaty-based and its customary (or undressed) strains. Now we move to my third of four proposed causes for the diminishing scope for democratic decision-making in our five countries – five of the very oldest democracies in the world.

Here we will consider supranational organizations. Before doing that, however, ask yourself this question: Does democracy work, or work well, above the level of the nation-state?

Recall from the preface that I mean by "democracy" the morally unvarnished, thin notion of letting-the-numbers-count majoritarianism. Within the boundaries and governing arrangements of the nation-state we can all understand how democracy works, at least in basic terms. Yes, there will be plenty of diversity in the sense that looking across the democratic world some countries will have parliamentary systems and others presidential ones; some will have only one functioning legislative chamber and others two; some will be constitutional monarchies and others republics; some will have floating election dates largely at the discretion of the party in power, others will have fixed election dates; some will be federal systems with powers divided between the centre and the states (or provinces or länder or cantons), and others will have a unitary rather than federal set-up; most will have bills of rights, though not Australia, and though some will not be justiciable in the courts and some again will be statutory rather than entrenched in the constitution; and of course there will be a bewildering array of voting systems on offer from the long-established FPP system of the UK, United States, and Canada through the preferential or alternative vote system in Australia (where voting is also compulsory) to PR voting systems such as single transferrable voting in Ireland and the closed list mixed member proportional system in Germany and New Zealand.

So yes, the diversity of democratic arrangements can be quite staggering as different countries opt for different choices from the possibilities on offer in the preceding paragraph. Yet all that diversity and all those differences sit on top of a basic reality – that it is the people who are citizens (in some countries) or permanent residents (in others) who get to vote for representatives to resolve a host of contentious social policy line-drawing decisions that need deciding. In other words, the basic currency is living, breathing human beings; it is individuals who will vote and who, in sufficient numbers, will comprise the majority and have their preferences prevail and their value judgments legislated into law.

Leave the nation-state behind for bigger waters, however, for the supranational world of EU or United Nations decision-making, and it's not at all clear whether democracy can work, or even be used as an appropriate term to describe what is going on. At the United Nations there is certainly voting, but it is voting by nations and countries. And there are vetoes by any one of five historically powerful countries.

The EU also has plenty of voting. Much of it is by countries; some of it involves opt-outs; much of the country voting is weighted and requires what is quaintly described as a "qualified majority."[45] In the recent past when the draft EU Constitution was being considered some of the constituent countries allowed their citizens to vote on it in a referendum, but when majorities said "no" in France, Holland, and Ireland the United Kingdom decided not even to consult its voters. And when that draft constitution was repackaged and rebranded as the "Lisbon Treaty," even though it retained some 99 per cent of the content from before, the French and Dutch opted not to ask their voters a second time, and the UK, again, not to ask at all.

Clearly, then, democracy is at best a very different animal in the supranational context than it is at the level of the nation-state. Voting by countries – whether on a veto or qualified majority or regular majority basis – is not the same thing as voting by individual people. Of course you can take "votes by countries" and try to translate what is happening into "votes by people" terms. What you end up with is not majoritarianism, as a single country with lots of population can lose to a collection of countries with small to medium populations. At most you might think of it as a sort of US Senate–style version of democracy, where countries with big populations get the same representation as do far littler ones.

Even that, however, is misleading. At the level of the United Nations there are plenty of non-democracies, even one or more veto-wielding ones. No one knows for sure what the majority thinks in these regimes as people are never asked.

The EU, by contrast, is a club for democracies, twenty-seven of them at the time of writing. But it is not a club where these constituent democratic national states have a vote on everything. It is much more in the nature of a bureaucratic superstate. The European Commission is basically an unelected civil service, an extremely powerful civil service. It is this Commission that proposes new EU laws. No individual citizen of a member country even gets to vote for the EU president, or any of the other top Commissioners. The jobs are stitched up by deals among the twenty-seven member states, and these intergovernmental deals are subject only to a full-slate up- or-down veto in the hands of the Parliament. This amounts, at most, to an indirect veto power in the hands of that European Parliament.

It is not controversial to say that if this model were reproduced at the level of the nation-state, any national state, no one would call it democratic. It smacks more of a sort of Hong Kong compromise where the attempt is made to give a facade of democratic respectability to what is democratically deficient and wanting beneath the surface – though that comparison is admittedly unfair to Hong Kong where individual voters have more direct input, a lot more, than they do into EU law-making.

Even the elected EU Parliament itself seems deficient, and not simply because it does not propose laws but can only veto or vote them down. There is also a sort of absence of accountability when it comes to this Parliament. It can vote down Commission-proposed laws, as I've just noted, but it does so without any risk of bringing down the EU government and triggering new elections. And voters have no sense of what they'll end up with when they vote, which may or may not help explain the very low voter turnout to EU Parliament elections. Put differently, party politics is more or less meaningless. It's not just that supposed left-wingers from Sweden are more pro-free trade than supposed right-wingers from France, or that no one has any notion of how the political party one votes for will fit into some later EU-level coalition. No, it's more that the lack of real democratic input and democratic power results in a sense that little is at stake, that no competing ideas about the economy, or world affairs, or how to balance welfare and rights concerns, or anything else, are being argued over to see which ones will prevail in the court of public opinion, and then be implemented.

Yet all that has to do with the nature of the EU project itself. I think that project, despite being a club for democracies, is not itself run in a way that anyone (at least if it were mimicked at the nation-state level) would describe as democratic.[46] If not innately or inherently anti-democratic, it is certainly democratically deficient; it is too full of Eurocrats who often sound condescending and hostile to democracy; and it has too often run scared of making its case to the people of the EU and being governed by their verdict. It is a top-down, elitist-built work, one in which referenda were avoided where possible when the transfer of power to Brussels was at stake (just think of how Germany adopted the euro currency despite a clear majority of Germans wanting to keep the deutschmark) and if one was held and lost then it would be re-held until the desired answer was given (look at Ireland, including as regards the Lisbon Treaty).

All of that is true, I think, but it is only tangentially relevant to our concerns in this book. Equally tangential is the truth that this EU superstate, however bureaucratic, top-down, and lacking in terms of democratic input, has done some good things such as creating a single market and absorbing post-Soviet-collapse Eastern European states, as well as some bad things like forging the Common Agricultural Policy (CAP) that impoverishes many in the poor part of the world. Our concerns are different than these: they lie with five of the oldest democracies in the world and with how democratic decision-making is in decline in all five, to varying extents. So our focus is at the level of the nation-state. We want to see how these supranational organizations enervate democracy at the national level; we are not directly concerned with the democratic credentials of these higher order or supranational organizations themselves, though as I mooted at the start of this section it is an open question whether such bodies or organizations can ever be democratic in any full-blooded sense.

Now this focus on our five nation-states makes one thing abundantly obvious – this third cause of democratic decline affects the United Kingdom far, far more than it affects the United States or Canada or Australia or New Zealand. To the extent the EU is a sovereignty gobbling behemoth, it is only the UK of our five that is at risk.

So let's look at how this supranational EU, formerly known as the European Economic Community (EEC) and earlier still the European Coal and Steel Community (ECSC), affects what voters in the UK can decide for themselves by means of majoritarianism, of letting the numbers count, of electing representatives to a legislature to make laws that will be the last word in resolving all sorts of social, economic, and political issues.

The short, brief answer is that the EU is a sovereignty busting body. It takes all sorts of decisions out of the hands of the UK's elected legislature and places them up with the EU – decisions distributed in an often opaque way between the civil-service-like Commission that initiates laws, the Council (which you can think of as meetings of the twenty-seven heads of governments, plus Commission and Council presidents) that is often the real decision-maker (with fewer and fewer areas having national vetoes), and the Parliament whose members are elected every five years and that cannot initiate laws but can vote them down.

Since the *Factortame* decisions[47] by the UK's House of Lords (their then top court) in the early 1990s it has been clear and beyond doubt that domestic UK law loses to, or is trumped by, EU law whenever the two are inconsistent. Or rather that is the case right up to the point that the UK Parliament enacts a law to leave the EU, at which point the UK law prevails. (And the new Lisbon Treaty even sets out how member states can leave the EU, though in practice I doubt a powerful country like the UK that clearly wanted to leave would need to follow EU law on how to do so.)

This creates a rather massive democratic deficiency or gap in the UK that is unknown in the United States, Canada, Australia or New Zealand. Of course, in one sense it has a democratic imprimatur or legitimacy. Although the UK entered the European Community in 1973 under the Tory Ted Heath government, the Labour Party prevailed at the 1974 election promising a referendum on continued membership. That referendum was held in 1975, after Labour had renegotiated some of the entry terms, and support for EEC membership scored 67 per cent on a turnout of 65 per cent of voters.

In that sense then, of a majority at some point in the past voting to give up sovereignty, all of us can point to a source of democratic respectability for the UK situation today. That said, a good, solid democratic process for deciding to move to some new set of arrangements X and Y, in no way at all makes X and Y themselves democratic. A country's voters can vote fairly and openly to become a dictatorship or a theocracy, and that vote in no sense at all makes what they then have – the new dictatorship or theocracy – itself democratic.

I am not suggesting that the EU is a dictatorship or a theocracy. That would be ridiculous. But neither does it operate – at the supranational macro level – in sufficiently democratic or majoritarian or letting-the-numbers-count ways. In fact, as I have suggested, it often bends over backwards to avoid hearing what the majority thinks (in a particular country or as a whole across all twenty-seven of them). It produces and initiates laws from a committed bureaucracy, not an elected legislature. It takes important decisions (say, to adopt the euro) knowing it could not do so if voters were asked.

Having made that crucial point, that as an EU member UK law is trumped by EU law, I could also point out that the UK government can bypass its own elected legislature and as the executive just sign up to EU directives (limiting the work week, say, or opting in to the European Investigation Order granting much expanded powers to prosecutors from other EU states), directives that are hard and sometimes impossible later to get out of or jettison. In fact the way the government signed up to the Lisbon Treaty itself is a perfect example of a government locking in future generations to rules and arrangements that they cannot escape from, short of leaving the EU itself, and doing that without any election mandate (indeed all parties promised the opposite, namely *not* to do this without putting it to the people) or referendum victory.

For democrats like me, then, the situation in the UK is pretty depressing. And I say that, let me remind the reader, as someone who likes the single market and the effects (material and otherwise) on former Eastern Bloc countries now EU members, and probably even on countries like Ireland, Poland, and others (barring the euro crisis continuing its toxicity for a long, long time). Yet even conceding those good consequences, admitting there have been others, and wholly ignoring the travesties such as the CAP, there is still the rather large democratic deficiency or gap or absence the EU has brought with it to the UK.

For the UK, though not our other four countries, the EU is the largest cause of democratic decline. That is why I said near the start of this book that democracy had declined more there than in any of our other four countries.

However, as the EU is not a cause of democratic decline for the United States, or Canada, or Australia, or New Zealand, we should probably simply flag it as a uniquely potent or virulent cause for the UK, and then move on, trying to mask our unease about and dislike of the EU's democracy-debilitating tentacles as best we can.

There are, of course, supranational organizations that affect all democracies, including our five. There are the various subsidiary parts of the United Nations. Now the UN itself, in the sense of its General Assembly and Security Council, do not in any worrying sense at all impinge on democratic decision-making. Readers might think their respective country pays too much, or too little, into the UN coffers, but that is an altogether different issue. And it is one that must be considered in the context that some sort of organization of the world's countries is needed – and that such an admission does not prevent us from debating how bureaucratic it should be; whether non-democracies of theocratic or authoritarian hue can somehow be prevented from forming voting blocs; which countries, if any, ought to get a veto on the decisions of the others; and how, over time, those getting a veto might be changed in line with shifting economic, geopolitical and population changes, or anything else. None of those debates alter the underlying persuasiveness of claims that some sort of world body – some forum of nation-state governments – is better than none. In a world of nuclear weapons, ongoing industrialization, terrorism, possible epidemics if not pandemics, financial interdependence, and more, we need a forum and meeting place for nation-states. The details of how it is structured are open to massive debate. The need for some sort of UN or League of Nations is not, at least in my view.

But that is at the big-picture level, the one that will have few democracy enervating effects in Canada or the United States or Australia or the UK or New Zealand. The General Assembly is not likely to be voting to impose economic sanctions on any of our five countries, and even if we could force ourselves to suppose some wildly implausible scenario when it did, such sanctions would not receive the needed unanimity in the Security Council – for the obvious reason that two of its five members are countries we're considering.

That top echelon layer of the UN is not, then, a worry for us as we consider causes of democratic decline. What is a worry are some of the second-tier agencies of the UN, and more particularly the rights-related ones. Take today's UN Human Rights Council (UNHRC). This is an intergovernmental body, subsidiary to the General Assembly. In 2006 it replaced the UN Commission on Human Rights (UNCHR). The Council was created to replace the Commission because the latter was widely seen to be (according to taste) ineffective, overly politicized, controlled by voting blocs from the world's despotic regimes, anti-Israel, anti-American, or some combination of all of the above.

Now that the Council, the UNHRC, has been up and running since 2006 it is widely seen to be (according to taste) ineffective, overly politicized, controlled by voting blocs from the world's despotic regimes, anti-Israel, anti-American, or some combination of all of the above. Some think the Council even worse, even more dysfunctional, than its predecessor. Indeed under the George W. Bush administration the United States boycotted the Council, though that boycott was lifted by the Obama administration.

For our purposes in this book, the main feature of the Council's work to point to is the Periodic Reviews – where the Council assesses the human rights situations in all 192 UN member states.[48]

Leave aside the obvious observation that the world's Sudans, Libyas, Chinas, Zimbabwes, Cubas, Irans, and Saudi Arabias are comparatively unmoved by such Periodic Reviews. They might even get themselves voted onto the UNHRC – as Libya has, and Cuba has, and China has, and Kyrgyzstan has, and Pakistan has, and Saudi Arabia has, and, well, you get the idea – in order to hamper critical Periodic Reviews by forming voting or power blocs. But even if a Periodic Review does come out that is critical, the world's authoritarian and theocratic states pay little attention.

There is the great irony. The countries that clearly, undeniably, and obviously to all have the best records in according their citizens freedom to practice their religion, to speak and write and report without censorship, to associate and assemble as they please, and basically to enjoy the freedoms that go into any list of desirable enumerated rights will be the democracies. Democracies (on average, over time) accord citizens more freedom, more liberty, a better deal on human rights, put it in whatever terms you wish, than non-democracies. And the gap is somewhere between large and huge.

Worse than that, it is the world's democracies that pay more attention to these Periodic Reviews than the non-democracies. Now that would be fine in a world where the people appointed to undertake these Periodic Reviews had superior moral perspicacity or better moral antennae or some magical pipeline to God on all the contentious, debatable, open-to-reasonable-disagreement rights-related issues that come up when considering democracies. But they do not! They come from a narrow cross-section of legally qualified people and there is no reason at all to think their views on where to draw social policy lines related to criminal procedures, how to treat those claiming to be political (rather than economic) refugees, abortion, all the way down to corporal punishment issues are better than the views of the majority of Americans, or Canadians, or Brits, or

Kiwis, or Aussies. Top domestic judges in our five countries may at times treat the views of those who write these Periodic Reviews as more attuned with "best moral positions" (which, the cynic might add, you can read as "our moral positions as unelected judges"). But there are no grounds for thinking that to be the case, or no grounds that can be cashed out, generalized, and defended in across-the-board terms.

That means that every time a democratic country's judges or executive branch alters what would otherwise be its position due solely or largely to assertions made in one of these Periodic Reviews, democratic decision-making has been diminished.

Meanwhile the questions "Who gets appointed to staff these Periodic Reviews?," "Do their credentials make them better at spotting the rights-respecting course of action in cases where smart, nice, reasonable people simply disagree than the elected representatives of the people?," and "Why should we care what these Periodic Reviews allege?" simply cannot be answered in a way that favours these UN bureaucrats over elected politicians in our five countries.

Remember, the issues that come up for criticism in democracies are not ones of closing down the newspapers, of forbidding religious worship to minorities, or indeed to everyone, of stoning women to death for adultery, of organizing militias to butcher those in troublesome regions, or other really easy cases where virtually all of us would agree the chosen course of action was morally despicable. Those sort of easy cases are to be found in non-democracies – the places that pay no attention to Periodic Reviews, or that get themselves voted on to the UNHRC to form a bloc to forestall the worst sort of criticism.

I could more or less repeat myself at this point, and go on to say much the same sort of thing about the various committees that are set up to monitor the progress in implementing the rights-related multilateral treaties or conventions. But as I've already given you an idea of how that works above, with the case study on article 19 of the UN CRC and its alleged application to the spanking of children by parents, let me just claim that all these supranational organizations – the ones set up to pass judgment on how well democratic nation-states are respecting rights – are yet another cause of democratic decline.

To be as blunt as needed here, the people who staff these organizations and committees and councils have no greater moral perspicacity than the elected representatives certainly of our five old, well-established democracies. They bring no extra moral expertise to the table. And yet on the other side of the ledger they have obvious failings: they are not accountable for their decisions; they are not chosen in any transparent or acceptable way; indeed virtually no one knows who they are.

One supranational organization, however, does require further discussion in the context of the erosion of democratic decision-making. It requires that extra discussion because it is not a rights-related body, but rather a trade-related one. This is the World Trade Organization (WTO).[49]

The WTO grew out of GATT, or rather the General Agreement on Tariffs and Trade treaty. Immediately after World War II about two dozen countries participated in the United States propelled negotiations to cut tariffs. These negotiations were independent of the rather grander attempt, the failed attempt, to agree to the Havana Charter which would establish something that would be called the International Trade Organization or ITO. The sideline GATT negotiations were completed in the middle of 1947 and GATT was born on the first day of 1948. It was assumed it would be temporary, lapsing once the Havana Charter came into force.

However, when the United States, under President Harry Truman, decided not to pursue congressional approval for the Havana Charter, only the GATT was left. And GATT was not only a document assumed by all and sundry to be temporary, it was also a narrowly focused agreement aimed at lowering tariffs.

When supporters of sweeping powers for judges under bill-of-rights-type instruments try to make an analogy to GATT and the WTO remember this first difference. GATT and the WTO are ultimately focused on one thing, lowering (and perhaps one day even eliminating altogether) tariffs. That is their aim, focus and breadth of concern. It is a massively more circumscribed, contained and inflation-resistant one than some document (domestic or international) that is pitched up in the Olympian heights of emotively appealing and disagreement-finessing moral abstractions – one that enumerates a list of vague, amorphous, indeterminate moral entitlements in the language of rights and then hands it over to judges to interpret knowing full well, going in, that most such interpreting judges will be adherents of living-constitution or living-tree or living-bill-of-rights-type interpretive approaches that multiply the scope for the interpreting judge's own subjective moral sentiments to be relevant, and even decisive.

When it comes to making inroads into democratic decision-making, remember that first difference between the trade-related WTO and all the rights-related legal instruments (such as domestic bills of rights and international rights-related conventions and treaties) out there.

Returning to our brief historical account, GATT entered into force in 1948 and that was all there was for nearly half a century, until the WTO was established in 1995. Yet GATT still remains the most important legal document in international trade law. The WTO agreement that grew out of the Uruguay Round did *not* supplant or repeal the original GATT document; it merely complemented and supplemented GATT.

Here's the next thing to notice about trade agreements. Nation-states argue over every phrase, every word, every comma. In the history of the GATT there have been eight completed sets of rounds of Multilateral Trade Negotiations (MTNs), all aimed at reducing trade barriers. And these are increasingly difficult to complete – the Doha Round began in 2001 and is still yet to be completed – for the very fact that they emphatically do *not* deal in finessing disagreement under the cover of moral abstractions, vagueness and amorphousness. These trade rounds, to the contrary, deal in spelling out in minute detail specifics; they enumerate and elaborate with precision; they aim to make clear up front what countries have committed themselves to, and when; there is no sense of having aimed for the woolliest, least demanding lowest common denominator, with some countries possibly holding their noses and crossing their fingers behind their backs hoping some latter day judges will expand the reach of the articulated indeterminacies in ways they think morally best – which in obverse terms is to say that non-democracies have as much at stake as democracies, a situation wholly distinct from rights-related treaties.

Trade agreements, in other words, are driven by self-interest that flows from a grasp of comparative advantage, an understanding that free trade (*not* mercantilism) creates the new wealth that can later be allocated as different countries choose, and a recognition that greater trade does not much (contrary to some) reduce the power of domestic governments. And if you're in doubt about that last claim, take a visit to China some time, and experience for yourself how enfeebled, or otherwise, the Communist Party government of China is. This is the government that has signed China up to the WTO without any overly obvious inability to set domestic policy across the board.

My point here is that the WTO process is one obsessed with detail and trying to spell out probable future scenarios and commitments. It is one that aims to be a "no-surprises," up-front process. It confronts disagreement in order to generate trade-off compromises; it does not finesse disagreements for some later point-of-application interpreter to award the whole cake to one side or the other (as happens with rights-related judicial decisions over abortion, or same-sex marriage, say).

Consider the approach to these GATT and WTO negotiations. They take place on a "product-by-product" basis with a focus on reducing tariffs, and in the context of an overarching Most Favoured Nation (MFN) obligation found in article I of GATT. The general goal, as I have said, is to lower import barriers and to reduce export subsidies. The MFN obligation requires member states to give the same lower tariff deal or concessions to all other member states that they give to their most favoured member state trading party. Against that background and even though there are some exceptions to MFN treatment, you will see that this sort of trading regime dispenses with reciprocity – you can't demand something from country X in return for your lowering tariffs if you've already lowered them for any other WTO member country.

Again, nothing like that seems true of treaties and conventions related to, say, the rights of the child, or indigenous peoples, or the disabled. And so, also again, this WTO process is much less debilitating of democratic decision-making. In fact, any country can opt to leave the WTO, though none has done so.

An obvious issue with the WTO is dispute resolution and the power of those who resolve them. And yet again we see here that there are more constraints on the Dispute Settlement Body panels and Appellate Body than you find on regular (and likewise international law) judges deciding rights-related issues. First off, there is no enforcement mechanism the winners can use against the losers, other than being paid compensation or undertaking authorized retaliation (think of the EU's ban on genetically modified crops, which fails the trade test but that failure, or America's winning at the WTO, cannot easily be used to change the EU policy, which still exists).

Second, although there has been interpretive slippage in the WTO's Dispute Settlement Understanding process at the Appellate Body stage, it has been very slight and is pretty much Mickey Mouse stuff compared to striking down the elected legislature's abortion statutes, and marriage statutes, and criminal procedure statutes, and all sorts of other statutes even tangentially related to equality concerns or any of the other rights concerns. At the WTO we might see the Appellate Body allowing NGOs to submit briefs in cases or decide who has the burden of proof or even, very rarely, cite eminent publicists. But that's the scope of the slippage.

All of this means that those who attempt to paint trade-related supranational organizations as equally undermining of democracy as the EU or as rights-related supranational bodies and domestic judges have their work cut out for them. In fact, it is an impossible task. At the margins the WTO does affect democratic decision-making, no doubt. But almost all the constraints come in the form of highly detailed and specific undertakings, not in the form of disagreement-finessing abstractions. Or put differently, a democratic government in the past knew the exact detail – or rather almost all the detail – of what it was agreeing to. There is little of the ratchet-up effect we see elsewhere.

One may still ask why one generation (metaphorically speaking) ought to be able to lock in future generations, the question always asked of all written constitutions, but since the inroads on democratic decision-making are confined and few, and it is easy to leave the WTO, even that grievance is tempered. This is not a case of one generation writing a blank cheque which later generations will have to pay, the amount and payee altering over time as the living-document interpreters update and alter what the unchanging words mean.

Perhaps I should sum up in especially blunt terms. The WTO, as a supranational body, is much less democracy debilitating than rights-related supranational bodies. The deal is made up front. It is procedurally easy to back out. There is far less scope for inflation-enhancing living-document interpretive approaches by those who judge disputes. Those who breach their obligations face only the option of paying, or authorized retaliation. And widespread self-interest, in the form of the increasing generation of wealth, at least partly aligns outlooks. Oh, and *every* country has a veto on any changes – you need unanimity to change the bargain – which no one can say of the EU.

People worried about the decline of democracy, people like me, have much to worry about when it comes to the EU and to some of the ancillary UN bodies. They have next to nothing to fear from the WTO.

UNDEMOCRATIC ELITES

This section will conclude this part of the book. And it will be short. Here I point the finger at all those lawyers and self-styled human rights activists and special interest promoters and lobby group members and officials and bureaucrats and others who calculate that they will lose in the court of public opinion – that they will be unable to convince a majority of their fellow citizens to their way of thinking – and so prefer to do an end run around majoritarian politics. They prefer to put their case to a single federal court judge than to the people of California. They choose not to ask voters in the UK (or France) about a new EU Constitution, but to resolve that question behind closed doors. They ask New Zealand judges to read-in some previously unheard of "partnership" status for the Maori, rather than trust the elected legislature that was the world's first national one to grant women the vote and that gave Maori men the vote way back in 1867. They bad mouth and belittle any mooted use of Canada's section 33 notwithstanding clause (or override of the judiciary provision). They seek to overturn the wishes of a big majority of voters in Arizona. And the list goes on, and on, and on.

In effect, my use of "elite" connotes anyone prepared to impose his or her preference or sentiment or long thought-out value judgment on the country without bothering first to convince a majority of us that this preference or that value belief or this moral position is the best one (or least-bad one) in the circumstances. The "elite," in my sense, are all those who succumb to the temptation to bypass letting-the-numbers-count institutions in favour of putting their case to some committee of ex-lawyers (or to be exact, and this is deliciously ironic, to a majority of this committee of ex-lawyers because recall that the decision-making rule on all top courts is a purely procedural one – five awful, morally insipid opinions or judgments always and everywhere still beats four inspiring, morally profound ones, even where the latter remember to quote John Stuart Mill, the ICCPR, and Kant's categorical imperative). Or if not to the ex-lawyers on some top court, then to EU bureaucrats, or to international judges, or to law professors, or to those sitting on tribunals or some committee monitoring a convention or treaty.

These elites may be trying to stop parents legally spanking their children; they may be trying to legalize euthanasia, or abortion, or same-sex marriage, or (from the other end of the political spectrum) gun use; they may be aiming to liberalize the flow of people in and into Europe; they may want different labour-relations regimes, or a more equal (or indeed libertarian) treatment of people and groups; they may want to end capital punishment; they may see themselves as crusaders on behalf of indigenous or native peoples; they may want to emasculate anti-terrorism laws or campaign finance laws; it really doesn't matter what their aims or how they envisage their quest. If they willingly and happily look to non-democratic institutions to gainsay, second-guess and trump the country's elected institutions, then they are in my sense undemocratic elites. (So notice that in that sense even some members of the media can sometimes be classified as part of the undemocratic elite.)

And, also in my sense, that is not a good sort of elitist to be. It is that group that bets they can get more of their first-order preferences, values and policies satisfied by side-stepping the majority and asking the unelected judge, the unelected EU bureaucrat, the unelected law professor or convention monitor or publicist.

It is people just like those who have been a cause of the decline of democracy these past few decades in the United States, in New Zealand, in Australia, in Canada, and most of all in the UK.

Notice two further things. The first is that this loss of faith by these elites in the ultimate good sense, and judgment, and morality of the majority of their fellow citizens may, in fact, be the most fundamental cause of the decline I am lamenting. If this elite were steadfast in their attachment to democracy then the judges would be more deferential and far less interpretively adventurous, the supranational organizations would be forced to put issues to the voters, and international law would be kept within proper limits by the politicians.

And that last claim takes me to the second further thing, which is this. That "elite" group that has lost faith in democracy and majoritarianism, be it a little loss of faith or a lot, can and sometimes does include our elected politicians too.

It is elected representatives of the people in the UK who decided not to put the Lisbon Treaty to a referendum vote – and this despite the fact all three major parties went into the preceding election with a stated commitment to holding one. The excuse they gave that their commitment related to the draft EU Constitution, not to the Lisbon Treaty, was pathetic. The latter is just the former with a new name, a few peripheral matters removed, but 99 per cent of the content retained. Changing your girlfriend's name, and then having her cut her hair and buy a new outfit does not make her a different person, nor stop you from recognizing her on the street. Nor is it much better to say, "We can't give you a vote because it's too late now and (this next part *sotto voce*) we don't want needlessly to annoy the EU."

And it is Canada's elected parliamentarians who consistently refuse to invoke the section 33 notwithstanding clause, or judicial override provision, no matter how much they disagree (on rights-respecting moral grounds) with the Canadian Supreme Court judges who have struck down and invalidated one of their laws. Why is this? And why do some American legal scholars continue to point to this section 33 as evidence of greater majoritarian influence in Canada when that provision has never once been used at the federal level by Ottawa legislators – not one single time in the entire time since 1982 when Canada entrenched its US-style constitutional bill of rights? The elected government didn't use section 33 when the Court struck down prohibitions on tobacco advertising,[50] nor when it invalidated common law marriage definitions that had restricted that institution to opposite-sex couples,[51] nor when it gutted immigration laws,[52] and abortion laws,[53] and legalized medical marijuana,[54] and created a right of prison inmates to vote,[55] and the list goes on.

So Canada's elected members of Parliament, and those forming its Cabinets and governments, are even complicit in sponsoring rights-related and other litigation, on occasion not really trying to win those cases, while showing remarkably little backbone and willingness to defend democratic decision-making – and for this native-born and educated Canadian that is deeply embarrassing to admit. Politicians in the Great White North show nothing like the commitment to majoritarian resolution of contestable and contested social policy disputes that Antipodean politicians Down Under and in the land of the All Blacks regularly and still display. Australian parliamentarians, and New Zealand parliamentarians, have a confidence in democratic politics that Canadian parliamentarians have lost, or at least are not prepared to exhibit if it requires standing up to the top judges publicly.

Moving to the United States, we can see many elected officeholders there from president down through to those in Congress, to state governors, to elected mayors, who at times prefer winning their battles in the courts rather than in the court of public opinion. Elected politicians push or support court challenges to immigration laws, to marriage laws, to any practice that remotely seems to blend any aspect of church and state. They ask the unelected judges to second-guess, and invalidate, democratically enacted campaign finance laws, gun control laws, abortion restriction laws, and all sorts of anti-terrorism laws. And be clear that my grievance here is not that these laws are challenged in the courts – that's what comes with a strong judicial review American system; no, my grievance here is that it is often elected politicians who are the strongest supporters of these court challenges that seek to have laws struck down. They lost in the legislature and so they aim to win now in a counter-majoritarian or non-democratic forum. And the "they" are themselves elected representatives of the people.

Too much of this can foster a sort of two-facedness, or abdication of one's moral responsibilities as an elected official. It tempts one to take public positions one doesn't agree with, confident the judges would never condone such positions. So the public position becomes a freebie. It becomes, in one way, costless.

Take flag burning and laws that aim to make that a criminal offence. We all suspect – no, we all know – that there are some elected officials who have weighed the distastefulness and unpalatableness of burning the American flag against a conception of the proper reach or ambit of the criminal law in a democracy committed to liberty and freedom and who have decided (no doubt reluctantly and with a bad taste in the mouth) that it should *not* be criminalized. Yet some of these people will refrain from saying as much purely and simply because they are certain the US Supreme Court will strike down any laws aimed at criminalizing flag burning.

Some will even go further and publicly support such laws, and do so not because they want them enacted but rather because they know they will never be allowed to stand by the unelected judges.

The public position is a freebie. It's costless, or rather costless to them personally. The system allows for an unprovable sort of hypocrisy. It diminishes the link between supporting a new law and having to take responsibility for its effects. And surely this is one of the downsides of the American constitutional set-up, with its hyper-powerful judges, that often flies under the radar. When you as a Congress man or woman think you have philosopher-king judges standing behind you wielding the authoritative last word, you can indulge in irresponsible conduct. You can take positions you would not otherwise take. You can hush up what you perceive to be real failings in a proposed law. And you can do all that even if your view that the top judges are a sort of philosopher-king caste is overstated, or even downright misleading, or palpably false.

The noted Harvard Law School professor Lon Fuller, way back in 1949, wrote a short, entertaining but powerfully insightful article in which five make-believe, or mock hypothetical, judges in a pretend jurisdiction thousands of years in the future each issued an opinion on an issue at the borderline between law and morality. The idea was to explore what judges might do when their sense of moral rightness and justice pointed one way, and the seemingly clear words of the law pointed the other. Into the mouth of one of his five fictional judges, Justice Keen, Professor Fuller put these words:

> Now I know that the line of reasoning I have developed in this opinion [deciding the law should stand] will not be acceptable to those who look only to the immediate effects of a decision and ignore the long-run implications of an assumption by the judiciary of a power of dispensation. A hard decision is never a popular decision. Judges have been celebrated in literature for their sly prowess in devising some quibble by which a litigant could be deprived of his rights where the public thought it was wrong for him to assert those rights. But I believe that judicial dispensation does more harm in the long run than hard decisions. *Hard cases may even have a certain moral value by bringing home to the people their own responsibilities toward the law that is ultimately their creation, and by reminding them that there is no*

principle of personal grace that can relieve the mistakes of their representatives.[56]

That sentiment is expressed from the vantage or point of view of the judge. But it can apply just as much from the vantage of the elected representative. We need our elected politicians to fight their battles outside the courts – battles over what is best to do where both sides are aiming for what they think best, disagreement being normal and, indeed, between smart, well-informed, reasonable people and not a sign of wickedness, moral turpitude, stupidity or the need for re-education by all those opposed to your particular views. If our elected representatives aren't steadfast in fighting their battles in the realm of democratic legislatures and elections, who will be? If their instinct is not to shun the courts, whose will be?

And what of elected American politicians who refuse to defend in court the laws that exist on their statute books, preferring to have judges remove them undemocratically in the course of litigation rather than make the arguments that would pave the way to their being repealed in the elected legislature?

Other examples of elected representatives circumventing majoritarian institutions abound. In Australia the prime minister and Cabinet sign up to international treaties to get their way in federalism disputes with the states or to lock in future governments from the other side of politics. In Canada special advice-seeking reference cases are put to the Supreme Court, ones that sometimes are poorly disguised attempts to preclude future democratic choices. In the UK governments on occasion drive policy surreptitiously through the EU, driven by a fear of attempting to do so openly and by means of domestic democratic politics. And in the United States some politicians applaud a UN report critical of the immigration policies and laws of the elected state government of Arizona.[57]

Whatever the extent of this hollowness in the commitment to democracy among the politicians of our five countries – and my personal view is that Antipodean elected officials compare favourably on this score against those from our three northern hemisphere countries, though American ones are surely best of the latter lot – it clearly exists. That means that my category of undemocratic elites who are a further (and fourth) cause of democratic decline is a category that sometimes includes our democratically elected lawmakers themselves.

All of us supporters of letting-the-numbers-count democracy need to hope that this resignation or hollowness or sometime lack of faith in democratic institutions that appears to be felt by some of our elected politicians does not grow and become more widespread. We need to hope it contracts. Maybe then the other elites who even more obviously and vociferously prefer the courts and international bodies and supranational institutions and reliance on living-tree interpretations of international law to the hard work involved in persuading their fellow citizens, or a majority of them, over to their way of thinking will be a tad more hesitant to employ the various end runs around democracy they currently employ.

It certainly couldn't hurt.

PART THREE

Complications Masking Decline

I want now to shift our focus away from the causes of democratic decline and onto the way that decline can be, and often is, masked or disguised. Some of this ground I touched on briefly at the very start of this book, in the preface. Still, it is worth returning to these tactics or ploys – be they honestly subscribed to, or not. It is worth doing so to try to answer this question: "Why isn't the decline of democratic decision-making more widely publicized or discussed or condemned or lamented?"

Remember, no one doubts the fact that our five democracies have differing initial commitments to the extent letting-the-numbers-count majoritarianism will resolve contentious, debatable social policy line-drawing disputes. As I made abundantly clear in part I of this book, the very trusting New Zealand–style set-up with no written constitution, only one legislative chamber, and no federalism lies at one end of the "put your faith in the voters" spectrum. Australia comes close to that, with a written constitution that overwhelmingly leaves things to the elected legislatures, federal or state.

The United States in some ways looks more distrusting of majoritarianism than any of our other countries, with its strong commitment to a powerful upper-house Senate where voters in relatively unpopulated states are worth a good deal more than in big, populated states, and especially to extremely powerful judges who can gainsay and second-guess the elected legislative and executive branches. In other ways, though, the United States puts more trust and emphasis than anywhere else on voters and elections and majoritarianism – think of the incredibly wide array of official positions that you can only hold by winning an election there and the wide spectrum of views that can find an outlet thereby making it so much harder for a one-size-fits-all elite consensus or orthodoxy to capture all the viable electoral vehicles on certain issues and so overrule majority sentiments, and even the way mobility and decentralized decision-making allow for more individual preferences to be satisfied.

All of that, and the rest of the differences between our five countries when it comes to their starting-point commitment to majoritarianism, I discussed in part I of this book. And I did that not just because it is plainly correct that no two of our five countries had the exact same initial commitment. I did it too in order to lay the groundwork for this book's core claim presented in part II, that democracy is in decline in all five of the countries I'm considering. Democratic input is declining in the United States, and in Canada, and in the UK, and in New Zealand, and in Australia.

Whatever the initial starting point and commitment to democratic decision-making, there is less than there was a few decades ago. The trend is bad everywhere. Sure, it's worst in the UK. And Canada doesn't look great either. But the United States, Australia and New Zealand are also seeing a decline in the extent to which contested social issues are resolved by majoritarian processes.

At any rate, that was the claim I defended in part II of this book.

In part III, I will speculate on how that decline has been disguised or masked. I will offer up a series of responses or ploys that have been, and are, used to mask that decline.

PLOY #1: ALLEGE "YOU'RE WRONG ON THE FACTS, ALLAN"

Here the ploy is a simple one. You just say I'm wrong on the facts. So unelected judges, you claim, are not adopting ever more expansive approaches to interpreting bills of rights. And international law is not increasingly intruding into the scope for democratic decision-making (or if it is, then with some quick and fancy footwork you shift to saying that international law itself has solid democratic credentials and a passable genealogy).

Likewise, you insist that supranational bodies are not eating into the overall extent of decision-making at the national level when it comes to our five old, well-established democracies. When it comes to the United Kingdom and the EU, of course, anyone who could make that sort of claim with anything approaching a straight face ought to move immediately to Hollywood and look for acting work.

But you get the general idea of how this first masking ploy works. It's just that this ploy is wrong; it's factually incorrect. Supranational organizations *are* encroaching on majoritarian decision-making, as *is* international law. And international law does *not* come with good, solid democratic credentials. Far from it, in fact. As for the top judges in our five countries, speaking here in terms of generalities over time, and it *is* clear that ever more of them appear ready to adopt expansive interpretive approaches that have the effect of leaving them with fewer external constraints on what result they can reach. Yes, yes, all proponents of such seemingly unfettered living-constitution or "progressivist" approaches tell us they often struggle in their minds, and that they *feel* constrained to go one way rather than another. But from the citizen's perspective that sort of constraint seems pretty insubstantial and not external to the values and sentiments a particular judge brings to the table.

Put differently, if it's all down to feelings and feeling constrained, why should an ex-lawyer judge's feelings count for more than a secretary's, or a plumber's, or a teacher's, or a pastor's, or even a bond trader's? After all, the practical effect of a judge's felt constraints will determine whether he or she overrules the elected legislature on issues such as same-sex marriage or capital punishment or abortion. At least that's what the constraints seem to amount to – to what the judge feels is right or best – under some of the expansive interpretive approaches becoming ever more fashionable and accepted.

To see a real, solid expansion of democratic input in any of our five countries you have to go back to the 1960s, and the civil rights movement in the United States. But that was fifty years ago. It only is relevant in the United States, not in any of our other four countries. Ironically, and this will infuriate some, it was legislation like the Voting Rights Act at least as much as (and arguably more than) US Supreme Court decisions such as *Brown v. Board of Education*[1] that dismantled the segregation that helped restrict democratic input. And the trend has been the other way ever since, with the scope for democratic decision-making and majoritarian resolution of contentious, debatable social policy issues in decline.

The first ploy is a dud. The facts point to decline.

PLOY #2: POINT TO THE FAILINGS IN DEMOCRACY

Decline is disguised here by focusing on democracy itself and then holding what one sees in real life up against some perfect ideal. When the actual democratic system in place in the United States or the UK or Canada or Australia or New Zealand then fails to meet the test of perfection, as is inevitable, it tends to escape notice that the field of play for these admittedly imperfect arrangements has shrunk. At the margins some less democratic alternative such as decision-making by judges or by supranational organization or in accord with international law has taken its place.

Now no partisan of democracy of whom I am aware, and certainly not me, thinks that any democratic system on earth is flawless or perfect. Indeed there is not even any agreed set of criteria about what is the best or most perfect set of democratic arrangements. People disagree. Smart, well-informed, reasonable, nice people disagree.

So nowhere is perfect, and besides, all of us differ on what perfect would look like anyway.

That means all of us can play the "criticize democratic institutions" game. Perhaps we can indulge in public choice theory speculations, pointing to the role of self-interest in the actions of our elected representatives and of the voters themselves. Or maybe we can criticize the lack of direct democracy, meaning the use of binding referenda. Or, we can flip that over and criticize the over use of these direct democracy referenda (though that is only remotely plausible in a few jurisdictions such as California, or Oregon, or moving outside our five countries to Switzerland). We can lament the lack of populism or too much populism. We can even despair at the extent of gerrymandering in the United States.

Or perhaps we might focus on whatever voting system we employ. If it's a FPP one as in the United States, the UK and Canada, we can criticize the way it turns elections into two party battles – the "ins" and the "outs" – and treats small political parties so harshly, and means a party can win a majority in the legislature with under 50 per cent of the vote, sometimes well under.

Meanwhile if it's a PR voting system as in New Zealand (or most of Europe) we can despair at how small political parties winning 5, 6, 7 per cent of the vote have massively disproportionate influence and sway – often decisive sway – into who forms government and what its policies are. And we can criticize how much compromise takes place *after* elections with PR, during the after-election negotiations needed to try to form a government where no one party ever wins a majority of spots in the legislature by itself.

Or we can lament low voter turnout in all our countries where voting is voluntary. In Australia, by contrast, we can attack the compulsory voting system used there, perhaps on the basis it equates the votes of those who want to vote and those forced to do so.

Or, in a moment of more abstract contemplation, perhaps we could ask what a vote for candidate X actually means and whether it provides a mandate for this, that or any other thing?

Yet all of these various sub-branches of this second ploy (of looking only at the failings, or perceived failings, of democracy) skew things by never applying the same cynical acid to non-democratic institutions. We rarely see public choice theory applied to the judiciary. And rather than nitpicking about this or that less than perfect aspect of our letting-the-numbers-count democratic institutions, where is the straightforward, head-to-head comparison between the credentials of those elected institutions (voting system warts and all) and any other institutions such as the judiciary, or UN Human Rights Council, or some monitoring committee to some international convention, or anything else?

More to the point, however, is this. I say the last few decades have seen a decline in democracy, in the scope for democratic decision-making. And quibbling about this minor failing, or that one, or even a stream of them – whether warranted or not – is beside the point. It is irrelevant to whether we are in decline or not. It amounts to a diversionary ploy.

By all means let's improve our democratic institutions to more fully let them measure and express majoritarian judgments, views, sentiments and preferences. But singling out current failings in those institutions – perceived or real, contentious or widely agreed – ought not to divert us from the fact that democracy is in decline.

This second ploy, then, amounts to a diversionary tactic, nothing more.

PLOY #3: REDEFINE THE CONCEPT OF DEMOCRACY SO THAT DECLINE SEEMS TO DISAPPEAR

To make use of this third ploy you need to take refuge in philosophical abstractions. And make no mistake. This third ploy is very common indeed. Many people who prefer their governmental and constitutional arrangements to come with a generous helping of what in years gone by might be described as "aristocracy," at the same time refuse, openly, to say that some things matter more to them than democracy.

In order to continue, then, to claim to be on the side of democratic decision-making and to remain (or seem to remain) a partisan of democracy, they redefine the concept of democracy.

They build in some tests about outcomes, some moral requirements that the laws of any jurisdiction claiming to be democratic must meet, or rather that these people say must be met.

So as I said at the very beginning of this book, the very concept of democracy gets hijacked. No longer does it suffice to think of democracy in procedural terms – about *how* a government is chosen. No longer is the focus on whether those who govern have actually been chosen by the people, whether the majority does or does not get to choose who will resolve all the many highly contested and debatable social policy line-drawing disputes. Democracy stops being solely about letting the numbers count and assessing whether a country's institutions do, or do not, let them count (which, I concede, is itself a matter on which, quite often, smart, reasonable, well-informed people will disagree and differ).

What you get instead is a new, added-on extra dimension to the concept of democracy. The term, in this new way of thinking, now means a great deal more than just some procedural concern with majoritarian decision-making.

It is now a much more morally laden, morally pregnant, fatter term this concept of democracy. It now requires particular substantive outcomes; being a democracy and describing some country's system as "democratic" now carries with it something extra, an additional assertion that the laws passed and the decisions taken have reached a certain level of rights-respectingness, some usually unspecified level of moral acceptability.

The result of adopting this thick or fat or morally laden understanding of democracy is that instances will arise where some country that would count as a democracy if you asked only how its government was chosen no longer gets to claim that label. Perhaps it is seen by some to trample too much on individual rights, or to adopt policies that severely disadvantage a particular religion, or to nationalize some people's property without compensation, or to ignore the demands of equality.

This fat, substantive, morally pregnant understanding or conception of democracy entails this inescapable side effect. If a jurisdiction produces outcomes that the users of the label "democracy" consider not to be good ones – or, to put the point in less sweeping terms, that they consider to be out-and-out morally bereft or wicked ones – then it stops being counted as a democracy however good its credentials might be in terms of how the government and legislature were chosen. And that is so even if there were real secret ballots; no electoral fraud; no men with machine guns standing beside people as they voted; no government monopoly on television campaigning; no threats to those in districts and constituencies that do not vote in the winning party that their roads and sewers will never be fixed; no swingeing defamation laws that make criticism of the government of the day near on impossible; in short none of the things that might throw into doubt whether the majority really has spoken in this election and whether we really can say we have let the numbers count; those issues aren't the only focus or concern.

For subscribers to this substantive, morally laden account can still withhold the label "democracy" from a jurisdiction provided they happen not to like what the majority is doing (or, at least, to think what the majority is doing is especially bad or misguided or beyond the Pale).

Think of it this way. Users of the word *democracy* who opt for this fat, morally pregnant usage want it to convey two things. The first is a claim about *how* decisions are made. The second is a claim about the goodness, or not-too-badness, of those decisions. Put in more straightforward terms, on this substantive, fat understanding, "democratic" is a description *both* (1) that decision-making is being done by some acceptably majoritarian process *as well as* (2) that the decisions actually made pass some pre-established moral threshold.

Of course there will be borderline cases when it comes to evaluating issues related to points (1) and (2). Well-informed, smart, reasonable people will simply disagree, on occasion.

Yet notice what follows from blending together the "is this a majoritarian process" issues and the "do the decision-makers follow nice, liberal, rights-respecting paths" issues. What follows is this. It becomes extremely hard to say "that country over there is a democracy, but in this instance it is doing very wrong-headed, even wicked, things."

Once you've turned the idea of "democracy" into the thicker, more substantive idea of "liberal democracy," you eliminate much of the room you would otherwise have for keeping separate the issues of how a country makes its key decisions (by letting the numbers count, or not) and of whether some, all or most of us think those decisions are usually or overwhelmingly freedom-protecting or autonomy-enhancing or rights-respecting or morally palatable (or acceptable on any other substantive basis).

That, in my view, is a mistake in its own right, and I say that knowing many people indulge in it. I think there are solid consequentialist grounds for wanting to leave yourself room to admit democracies can on occasion do bad things, even if you also think, like me, that the empirical record is abundantly clear that they do bad things far less frequently than non-democracies do.

Whether you agree with me on that point, or not, is not directly relevant to my central claim in this book that democracy is in decline. But notice what is relevant to that central assertion of mine. It is this. The fat, morally pregnant understanding of democracy makes it far more difficult for anyone to claim that the scope for democratic decision-making is being eroded, that it's in decline.

Why is that so? It's because the fat, morally pregnant crowd have turned democracy into a two component thing. For them it's now a (1) *and* a (2) stage affair. And that means no matter how much evidence I can bring to bear showing that (1) is in decline, perceived improvements in (2) outcomes (however fundamentally contestable and disagreement-provoking it may be to pass judgment on those outcomes) can be said to counter-balance the drop off with respect to (1).

So as I noted at the very start of this book, if I point to the EU and claim far too many decisions are made by a coterie of unelected bureaucrats, and even by national leaders in a way completely shielded from any accountability to the voters, proponents of a fat, thick conception of democracy can counter by pointing to what they claim are the substantively good outcomes produced by such decision-making, say the single market or the free flow of people, and so have room to deny democracy is in decline.

It is a neat trick. You can play it with over-powerful judges, with the UNHRC, with inroads made by international law, with just about anything.

When it comes to conceptions of democracy, the fatter they are, the harder it is to make them fall victim to claims of decline. You end up arguing not just about *how* decisions were made (namely, the procedures that lead to who gets to decide), but also about *what* was decided (namely, the moral acceptability of laws and outcomes). That means it's far tougher to argue that when Californian or federal judges overrule the elected legislature on same-sex marriage that this is an inroad into democracy; at least it's harder to do this to that half of the population that thinks such overruling is substantively (if not procedurally) justified. Or rather that's the case if they happen to think that the concept of democracy, in part at least, requires outcomes to be socially just ones – a very different notion, by the way, than thinking that majoritarian procedures *tend* (on average, over time) to do this more often than any other way of deciding issues.

This third ploy, then, is a sort of sleight-of-hand tactic. It ignores or pushes out of view the fact people disagree about substantive moral issues (see ploy #5 on page 138). More fundamentally, however, it simply attempts to redefine democracy so that any problems related to decline become so much harder to make.

We can wholly neutralize this ploy #3 in this way. We can put to one side our preferred meaning of the term *democracy*, and say instead that decision-making by the people – where each of us is counted more or less as equal to all the others and we all have a say in choosing those who will decide, the majority's choice prevailing until the next election – is in decline. That sort of commitment to letting the numbers count is in decline.

I happen to think that is best described as democratic decision-making. This ploy #3 muddies the waters by focusing on what is meant by democracy, and on contesting the best understanding of that concept. At the end of the day, of course, we can put that whole question of how best to understand the term *democracy* to one side, if need be. Your and my and the average voter's input into decision-making is being eroded by the expanding power and reach of judges, of international law, of elites, of supranational organizations.

This is in decline. What you call it is, in a way, neither here nor there.

This third ploy fails too.

PLOY #4: SAY, UNDER YOUR BREATH, "OTHER THINGS SOMETIMES MATTER MORE TO ME THAN DEMOCRACY"

We can deal very briefly with this fourth ploy. We can be brief because saying some other things matter more to you than majoritarian democracy is not a ploy. Lots of people want their democracy tempered by trade-offs in favour of federalism, say, or by a strong bicameralism where voters for that upper legislative house are in very, very unequally populated districts (such as Wyoming versus California), or even by a powerful judiciary interpreting a morally charged bill of rights.

That reality is why I began this book in part I by considering the different starting points – the differing initial attachments to majoritarian decision-making – in our five countries.

Remember, my complaint about decline is not an absolutist one. It's a relative one. Whatever the starting point (and they differ in New Zealand, Australia, the United States, the UK, and Canada), the trend is downwards.

So the ploy here does *not* involve simply admitting that some things matter more to you, at least sometimes, than letting the majority's view prevail. Lots of people think that, including most Americans.

No, the ploy here has to do with one's response to the fact of decline over the past few decades. I say that whatever the starting-point commitment to majoritarian, to letting-the-numbers-count decision-making in our five countries, the scope for that sort of democratic resolution of issues has in all of them shrunk, narrowed, shrivelled, contracted, diminished, decreased, call it what you will. That's the trend in recent years.

Now in response to that relative decline, that downward trend, it is of course possible that someone could say, "I always thought there was too much democratic input in my country (whatever the starting point), and so I welcome this new trend. I like, say, the fact judges are using a new living-constitution interpretive approach that magnifies their ability to gainsay and overrule the elected branches. And I like it because I'm not just agnostic about the benefits of democracy, I positively value some other things more than I do democracy."

Personally, I would not agree with anyone who made such an open, honest assertion. I think they're wrong on the consequential benefits of democracy. But that's a debate worth having and disagreeing with me on the issue in no way whatsoever amounts to a ploy, or a technique for disguising or masking the decline I point to. That's just a difference of opinion between well-intentioned, concerned people.

What does constitute a ploy, though, is thinking other things matter more but not admitting it openly and honestly. And surely a good many people do exactly that. They welcome the judges' intervention in California, the EU's intervention, well, on a myriad of fronts, and the ever greater role of international law. And they welcome it precisely because they care more about what these inroads achieve, or might achieve, than they care about democratic participation in government.

But they never say as much honestly and openly. They pay lip service to democracy, while welcoming this non-democratic inroad or that. And therein lies the ploy. It's the unwillingness to lay your cards on the table and defend your lack of trust in the core views of your fellow citizens that helps disguise or mask the decline. It's the preparedness to carry on as though the starting-point commitment to democracy in your country – whether it be the New Zealand one or the American one or one of the others – is one you still share, when you in fact no longer do. You welcome today's more restricted role for democratic decision-making.

Not being prepared to admit as much is a sort of ploy; it's a way to mask what's happening.

PLOY #5: GLOSS OVER THE FACT OF MORAL AND POLITICAL DISAGREEMENT IN SOCIETY

The trick here is to paint a world in which there is less disagreement and less dissensus than there really is. The more you paint a picture of "we are the world," lovey-dovey consensus and agreement, the less need there is for some procedure to resolve such disagreements – say one where you start by counting everyone as equal and then let them vote for representatives who will decide such contentious, debated, disagreed about issues.

As procedures go for resolving deep-seated social disputes, that one looks better than any other. Not perfect. Just better than any other option. It starts by counting us all equally. It gives an answer to the dispute only for so long as the majority view or judgment continues to point that way after regular elections. It is easier for those on the losing side to swallow their defeat, knowing it's a defeat only for so long as they fail to convince a majority of their fellow citizens that they are right and their opponents wrong. So it encourages civic participation.

But all this only makes sense if there are intractable social policy disagreements in our countries of 320 million or 65 million or 33 million or 22 million or 4 million people. Democracy, after all, is for us a thin, unvarnished, procedural tool for resolving such core social disagreements – about abortion; capital punishment; who can marry; how to balance public safety against the desire for criminal procedures that massively lessen the likelihood of convicting the innocent; how to structure immigration laws; when guns can be carried; what is the best balance between free speech concerns and, say, health and safety ones, or hate speech ones, or taking some money out of elections ones; whether convicted and incarcerated prisoners can vote; and so on and so forth.

Accordingly, our fifth ploy for disguising the decline in democracy involves downplaying disagreements. After all, there's no big reason to worry or obsess about the shrinking scope for democratic decision-making if talk of disagreement is overblown.

And here the roads diverge. Go down one path and you accomplish that trick of downplaying dissensus by suggesting most disagreement is unreasonable, that those who differ do so in bad faith or from impure motives.

I give that path its own category, and consider it separately as ploy #6 on page 140.

Here we will restrict ourselves to the path that tries to minimize the existence of disagreement in society rather than the one that agrees it exists, but characterizes it in terms of the moral failings of everyone who happens to disagree.

To recap, then, democracy looks more needed the more you concede that on a host of crucial political and moral issues there is disagreement in society. Smart, nice, reasonable, well-informed people differ on how to handle terrorists and would-be terrorists, on protectionism for farmers, on how to respond to genocide in far-off authoritarian regimes, and all the issues noted above. Admit this and you need a way to resolve those disagreements. Admit this and democratic decline is at least potentially a worry.

This fifth ploy disguises that decline by sweeping such disagreements under the carpet. It downplays them, minimizes them, pretends they aren't really there.

PLOY #6: INDULGE IN PROMISCUOUS CHARGES OF MORAL FAILINGS, BIGOTRY, RACISM, AND THE LIKE AS MOTIVATING YOUR OPPONENTS' ARGUMENTS

This sixth ploy follows on from the fifth one just discussed. Here the ploy is to paint all or most disagreement as unreasonable, motivated by bigotry or racism or defective moral antennae or the need for re-education or anything that characterizes those who disagree as beyond the Pale. Once that is accomplished, and all or most observed disagreement is put down to bad faith or stupidity, and you end up with a world where there is just agreement. At least you sort of end up there because the implicit message is that none of us need concern ourself with that sort of disagreement.

And as with ploy #5 above, if you lack the culture wars, the differences over committing troops, the blue state–red state divide, the battles over abortion and euthanasia, the freedom versus equality debates, the stay-in or get-out of the EU arguments, indeed most disagreement, then who needs to concern himself or herself much about a decline in democracy? Who cares, really?

Of course this sixth ploy is worse than its near relative, the fifth, because of the way it needs to attribute bigotry or general bad faith to one side of what would otherwise be some perceived disagreement. And, of course, it's always the *other* side. No one ever supposes that he is morally deficient, or racist, or in need of re-education. It's always the other fellow.

That sort of promiscuous indulging in the attribution of unworthy motives to those who differ and disagree is heard all the time. Just think of the same-sex marriage debate. The abortion debate. The Iraq War debate. The Keynesian stimulus debate. The health care debate. The list is never ending.

The temptation to indulge in ploy #6 is so great that many people are unable to resist it. Few recognize that a corollary to such allegations is a sort of puffed-up, self-righteous, sanctimonious bag-of-windness in the person casting such aspersions.

This ploy not only frees its user up from having to listen, think about, and respond to her opponents. It also makes it much less urgent to respond to my (or anyone's) claims that democracy is in decline.

Of all the ploys that mask and disguise democratic decline, this one bugs and bothers me the most. It is the one that is the most destructive of a well-functioning democracy where you listen, debate, try to convince, and yet often have to appeal to the procedural decision-making rule of voting and letting the numbers count. And you have to do that in good faith where you accept that those who disagree are as smart, as well-informed, as reasonable, as nice, as charming, as good company over dinner, and as everything else, as you yourself are. And it means you know going in that you will sometimes be on the losing side of these procedural resolutions of issues about which you care and feel strongly. Nevertheless, though, you know also that you don't get to scream "tyranny of the majority" or "racism" when that happens and you lose.

The underlying conceit that you are the culmination of 4.5 billion years of evolution so that your moral antennae quiver at just the right frequency and that you have some red-phone pipeline to God on all of society's contentious, disputed, debated issues is a conceit that can never be voiced openly and explicitly. Everyone would laugh at you, as everyone should.

I really detest this sixth ploy, though I concede it is in widespread use.

PLOY #7: PRETEND THAT STATUTORY BILLS OF RIGHTS DO NOT REDUCE THE SCOPE FOR DEMOCRATIC DECISION-MAKING

I have left this one for last because it only applies in a few of our countries. It is nowhere in existence in the United States or Canada, but only in the United Kingdom, New Zealand and sort of in Australia.

I refer here to the half-hearted attempts in the United Kingdom and New Zealand (and among those pushing for one in Australia) to claim that statutory bills of rights in no way diminish the power of the elected legislature. If that were true, then I would have been wrong back in part II of this book when I argued that these New Age statutory bills of rights do significantly decrease the scope for democratic decision-making.

But I wasn't wrong then. In fact I spent pages and pages explaining just how these non-constitutionalized instruments are very potent democracy-sapping things indeed. I pointed to the reading-down provisions they all have that tell judges to do all they possibly can to interpret all other statutes in a way they, the judges, happen to think is rights-respecting. I told the reader how the British judges have taken this reading-down provision to be a license that oh so fortuitously happens to grant them interpretation-on-steroids powers, or *Alice in Wonderland* ones, and have proclaimed that henceforth they can take the clear, unambiguous words used by the legislature (where the legislature's intention is also clear) and ignore both to give those words a new, different meaning (by reading words in and reading words out and redrafting things to reach what they, the judges, consider to be a rights-respecting final product).

If that isn't an inroad into democratic decision-making then I am a kangaroo. And though the New Zealand judges haven't gone as far as their rule of law enervating UK colleagues, they've gone far enough also to eat into the elected legislature's power.

On top of that I detailed how the judges operating these statutory vehicles also have a declarations power, one that in theory leaves the last word with the elected branches but in practice always, everywhere, sees the judges prevail.

And on and on I went in those pages earlier. Yet many, many proponents for, and defenders of, statutory bills of rights in these three jurisdictions continue blithely to mouth the refrain that these things are not diminishing and shrinking democracy; they continue doing this despite the empirical record and in seeming disregard of what I will describe as "the facts."

Of course it is a ploy, a pretense, to cloak and dissemble what many supporters and advocates of these instruments really know is going on. Either argue how it is that after a statutory bill of rights has been enacted the room for democratic decision-making has in no way been narrowed or impaired – an impossible task in my view – or come clean and admit what is happening and that you are in favour of that trend.

Pretending otherwise is a ploy to mask one particular cause of democratic decline (in some, not all, of our countries).

And saying that ends part III. I turn now to the fourth part of this book. This will be somewhat more speculative, and possibly depressing. It will, though, have the great virtue of being brief.

PART FOUR

Challenges Threatening More Decline

It is tempting to begin this final part of the book with a few more examples of inroads into democratic decision-making in our five countries. It is so tempting, in fact, that I am unable wholly to resist. I will, though, limit myself to examples from our two biggest, most important countries, the United States and the United Kingdom.

Start with the UK, not least because democracy is in the worst shape there of our five countries. As we have seen already, that is what happens when you opt to become a member of a supranational organization like the EU which is part superstate, part UN for democracies in one particular geographical region, and part ideal home for cosmopolitan, well-educated but unelected bureaucrats and administrators who seek to enervate national sovereignty in the name of various other goals such as political integration, the single market, a Common Agricultural Policy, a common currency, social democratic norms, and more.

And that is also what happens when you hand significant new powers to unelected judges under a souped-up statutory bill of rights known as the Human Rights Act, tied as it is to the European Convention on Human Rights.

But let me just mention two further instances of outcomes flowing from EU membership for the UK that appear unwanted by the majority of voters in the UK and, truth be told, not wanted by the majority of elected legislators in the UK.

One is the EU's "Working Time Directive," which has had significant consequences including over how doctors are trained and hospitals run. The elected UK government was unable to prevent this directive from being applied domestically and from trumping all domestic laws on the subject, though present Prime Minister Cameron did recently manage to negotiate a partial exemption, or opt out, from one (and only one) component of the directive – the forty-eight-hour work-week limit. But that limited exemption notwithstanding, democratic politics and democratic decision-making are the losers, or they are unless you happen to think that a democratic decision forty years ago to join the EU provides all future directives and rules emanating from there with an ongoing and full-blooded blanket democratic warrant. But I don't think that. As I pointed out earlier in this book, the democratic credentials of a decision to enter into a new governing set of arrangements is one thing, the democratic credentials of those new arrangements themselves once in place is another. In crude terms, the majority can democratically vote to live under a dictatorship or theocracy. But that does not make the newly put in place theocracy or dictatorship itself democratic.

Of course, I do not think the EU is a dictatorship. It is, as I have said, a club for democracies – a cross between a superstate and a weird sort of UN for the European democracies. But internally the EU is noticeably democratically deficient, and its decisions circumscribe the letting-the-numbers-count decision-making of member states such as the United Kingdom.

This working time directive is just one UK example of that democratic deficit.

Another is the even more recent example of Britain's acceptance of the European Arrest Warrant (EAW). This EAW requires almost nothing of other EU countries who request the extradition of UK citizens, and certainly not the normal prima facie evidence of a crime having been committed on their soil. The scope for potential abuse is certainly present and in mid-2010 about half of all those affected by it were being extradited from Britain. This, then, is another example of the same democratic deficit, since nothing the UK Parliament decides today (short of leaving the EU) can override it.

As I said, of our five countries things are worst in the UK. But we can cross from there to the United States and find further examples of inroads into democratic decision-making on the western side of the Atlantic Ocean too. They won't be as egregious as those in the UK, but that's hardly high praise or cause for self-congratulation.

Here is one that particularly irks me. It has to do with the State of Arizona and that state's 2010 immigration law, or rather immigration-enforcement law. In fact, it has to do with that law passed by the democratically elected state legislature, seemingly with much popular support in Arizona, and how the federal US government responded to that law.

Now the response that irks me, and that I think is another indication of democratic decline, is *not* the simple fact that the Obama administration disliked that Arizona law. Federal systems recognize that majorities who vote to put in place a national government and those (in some part of that nation) who vote to put in place a regional state government can be electing two sets of representatives who disagree. Indeed, that's not only to be expected at times, it's that disagreement that provides a main justification for having a federal system – after all, it's the competition that flows from disagreement that generally brings the downstream good consequences; having two bureaucracies and levels of government co-operate to do the exact same thing just adds another layer of costs and administration; so it's not often that co-operation is what brings federalism's good consequences; it's competition that does it.

Nor am I bothered by the fact the Obama administration sued the State of Arizona over this immigration-enforcement law,[1] the Justice Department's legal action alleging that it is the federal government (not the states) that has the authority to make and enforce these sort of immigration laws. Again, such disputes are part and parcel of any federal system. Along with distributing heads of powers to the centre and the regions, any federal system has to deal with the inevitable disputes that will arise when the two levels of government differ over who is authorized by the written constitution to pass laws that arguably do or do not fall under some head of power. In fact that is one of the core jobs of the top judges in a country with a federal system, to play the role of umpire in these disputes and decide between the claims of two democratically elected legislative bodies.

So what irks me is neither President Obama and his administration's dislike of the Arizona immigration law, nor the fact they managed to have much of that law struck down by the domestic courts on federalist grounds. No, what really bugs me about the Obama administration's response to that Arizona law, and what *does* amount to a creeping infringement or trespass on democracy and democratic decision-making, is this: It is that in late August 2010 the Obama State Department submitted a report to the UN High Commissioner for Human Rights, South African judge Navanethem Pillay. It was

America's first-ever such report, all earlier administrations having defended more vigorously America's national sovereignty and having refused even indirectly to give supranational organizations a say in this way over Americans and how they organize who can and cannot come into the country.

And this first-ever report was made in conjunction with what is known as the "Universal Periodic Review," suggesting or implying quite strongly that more reports will be coming. Moreover, in the course of this first- ever twenty-nine-page report, basically touting or looking for approval of various political policies (and let me stress they were contested policies not favoured by significant chunks of Americans), the report has a section on "values and immigration." And here the report basically singles out the Arizona law as being human rights deficient, notwithstanding the fact polls at the time showed a clear majority of Americans supported the law and notwithstanding that this is a contestable issue on which smart, nice, well-informed people can and do differ and disagree. The report apologizes to the UN High Commissioner for Human Rights and notes these failings are "being addressed in a court action,"[2] a predecessor to the one I just mentioned above.

My point here is not that this report is the worst sort of politically correct catalogue of what ought to count as a human right or human wrong, though readers could be forgiven for thinking of the report in those terms. No, my point is more fundamental, namely that a key purpose of making such a report is to acknowledge, if only implicitly and *sotto voce*, that this UN High Commissioner and the unelected bureaucracy under him have some legitimate say and influence over the highly contentious, debatable and disagreement-provoking issue of how best to structure America's immigration laws and how best to deal with those who enter the country illegally. There may even have existed a quiet hope that the UN General Assembly, based on this report, would condemn the Arizona law.

Whether that quiet hope existed, or not, no majoritarian democrat – at least not one like me – would say the UN High Commissioner has any legitimate role in resolving this issue. As this is a first ever report it is clear that no UN High Commissioner in the past had, or was implicitly acknowledged to have, a say. This was a new thing, a new concession.

However small or minute or at the margins, then, this is another example of the erosion and decline of democratic decision-making, this time in the United States. And, as with all the others, it is in my view to be regretted.

That said, and having now with these few examples from the UK and United States at least partially satisfied my temptation to indulge in more pointing and lamenting, let me move on to the more speculative task of suggesting what might in the near to medium future possibly portend or provoke further and greater erosions of democracy in our five countries, five of the oldest and most established democracies in the world remember.

Put more starkly, this last part of the book before I conclude will consider challenges that threaten even more decline and more erosion. As I said, it will be speculative.

Looking ahead, then, here are my speculations and musings on potential threats to democracy, be they at the margins or more existential and be they less or more likely to eventuate. Of course I don't pretend that my list of potential threats will be an exhaustive one, or even close to it.

The first challenge or threat I see comes from what I will describe as the attack on free speech. If the scope people have to speak their minds and say whatever they wish to say withers, then democratic decision-making is threatened. Perhaps not immediately. And perhaps not in any direct or 1:1 way. But even on my thin, procedural, unvarnished, "have we let the numbers count and the majority prevail?" understanding of democracy, voters need plenty of room to speak their minds and to be unencumbered in their attempts to persuade other voters to move to their way of thinking.

Why? Well John Stuart Mill answered nearly two centuries ago, when he gave his main ground for preferring very few limits indeed on what people can say.[3] "The peculiar evil of silencing the expression of opinion is, that it is robbing the human race; posterity as well as the existing generation; those who dissent from the opinion, still more than those who hold it. If the opinion is right, they are deprived of the opportunity of exchanging error for truth; if wrong, they lose, what is almost as great a benefit, the clearer perception and livelier impression of truth, produced by its collision with error."[4]

That answer points to the good consequences that, on average, over time, tend to flow from such a "leave people with lots and lots of scope to speak their minds" policy. Leave people almost always free to speak as they like and in the ensuing battle of ideas truth will out – or in more pessimistic terms, truth is more likely to emerge than if people are silenced, or silence themselves. So for the benefit of getting at truth and true assertions (and from there to the increased human welfare that generally flows from dealing with true rather than false information and inputs), we override hurt feelings, offended sensibilities, the possibility of outright lies being spread, the desire certain groups might have (understandably or not) to play the victim, and anything short of concrete harm to others.

Let me express that point slightly differently. Think about speech and its relation to offensiveness and downright falsehood. And then imagine a hypothetical spectrum. At the near end we have only actions and speech that everyone else (or almost everyone else) likes and thinks beneficial and correct. No one is offended by these actions and words. No one wants them silenced. At the other end we have the most offensive, obscene, untrue, and disliked actions and speech imaginable. Here, virtually everyone is offended; virtually everyone thinks the claims expressed to be untrue; virtually no one thinks the actions and words beneficial.

Now I take it that most readers will concur that at the near end of the spectrum, where all is agreement and harmony and people sitting in circles holding hands and singing "Kumbaya," there is no need for any institutional or popular commitment to widespread free speech. There is simply no need for it. Being free to say and do what everyone else wants you to say and do is not a freedom you or anyone will ever be in danger of losing or something you might need to fight for. And, by definition really, it will not apply to situations where people in society disagree and are arguing and are trying to convince others and will at some point need to invoke for society a procedural decision-making rule – say, counting everyone as equal and voting.

As for the far end of the spectrum, I am going to make an assumption. I am going to assume that no one is a complete absolutist who believes that in a society of 320 million or 70 million or 35 million or 23 million or 4 million there need be no limits at all on one's freedom to say or do as he or she pleases. At the very least, I will assume that we all agree on the need for government to prohibit (and then enforce that prohibition on) the counselling of murder, or the possession of child pornography (assuming further that we can agree on what this is). I will also assume that the vast majority of us likewise agrees about the benefits of limiting speech related to publishing true information about how to manufacture deadly and easy-to-make biological weapons or true information revealing the names of overseas government operatives working undercover where release of that information is likely to lead to these operatives being rounded up, imprisoned, and possibly killed.

My strong attachment to free speech, then, is not an absolutist or unconditional one. But it is a very, very strong one. I place myself a good way toward the far end of our imagined hypothetical spectrum and prefer, for example, the US defamation law regime to the UK one. (The latter gives more weight to protecting reputation when balancing that against free speech concerns.)

At the same time I recognize that when it comes to limiting free speech – to telling us where they would draw the line as far as preventing others from speaking or acting as they wish – different people fall at different points along our hypothetical spectrum. We disagree. Smart, reasonable, well-informed, nice people in society at large disagree, many of whom you'd be happy to share a drink with despite your disagreement.

That disagreement about where to draw the line is clear. But conceding all that is wholly consistent with being worried about emerging trends that seek to limit free speech.

The most obviously worrisome attempt along those lines is generally described under the banner or catch-all of "hate speech." Limits on free speech in our five countries under this banner of limiting "hate speech" is a serious worry – and it is a worry whether those limits come from the elected legislature (as until recently at the federal level in Canada, with its notorious section 13 hate-speech provision[5]), whether they pass muster with the highest judges in the land when asked to hold them up against a constitutionalized bill of rights' guarantee of freedom of expression (as in, again, Canada where the top judges are noticeably less protecting of free speech[6] than their top judicial colleagues in the United States), or whether they originate in UN offshoots that seek to restrict what individuals can say about religion.[7]

These sort of restrictions have long-term bad consequences for democracy because they take – or attempt to take – certain arguments off the table. They go some way toward creating a group right not to be offended. And they try to do this regardless of the truth of the uttered assertions. In fact, these sort of limits are desired most strongly against true assertions, or so it can appear.

Take this example. It is from a recent saga in Canada. On one side were the journalist and author Mark Steyn and *Maclean's* magazine, a weekly that had excerpted parts of Steyn's bestselling book *America Alone*. On the other side was the Canadian Human Rights Commission. That Commission, together with several similar ones at the provincial level, brought proceedings against Steyn and *Maclean's* for hate speech.

But here's the thing. This sort of hate-speech allegation did not require any assertion that Steyn's claims about immigration, Islam, comparative birth rates, or anything else were false. It was not necessary to sustain the case that Steyn was factually incorrect or in error in the excerpts *Maclean's* published from his *America Alone* US (and Canadian) bestseller. It could be hate speech anyway, or such was the basis for the proceedings.

And even though Steyn and *Maclean's* had the resources to call what turned out to be the bluff of these overly officious bureaucrats on this Commission, many others have not had those resources or the stomach for a lopsided fight where the complainers (read self-perceived victims) of hate speech have all of their legal costs picked up by the taxpayers – and can even be awarded five figure damage payments by the commission, to be paid by those they have complained against – but those pursued have to pay all their own legal costs (which in the case of Steyn and *Maclean's* was in the neighbourhood of $2 million).

It can be close to bankrupting to fight. Hence, even though Steyn and *Maclean's* ultimately prevailed in the sense that the Human Rights Commission dropped all of the proceedings against them (*not*, I emphasize, in the sense that Steyn and *Maclean's* received even a single penny of money to help cover *their* legal costs, because they didn't); and even though all my sympathies lie completely and without exception with Steyn and *Maclean's*; the fact remains that this hate-speech provision remains on the books in Canada as I write (though its repeal is imminent for the federal law, however not for the various similar provincial laws) and it continues to be the case that the leading Supreme Court of Canada precedents[8] hold that this provision does not get invalidated or struck down by the free speech right in the Canadian Charter of Rights – the irony of the top judges picking this sort of time to back-up democratic decision-making out of all the many choices on offer to them being stark! If it were part of a general deference to the elected legislature that would be one thing, and a good thing at that. But no one could accuse Canada's top judges of that sort of overall deference. So we inevitably end up in this type of "criticize when we disagree with the moral and political choices of the unelected top judges" game.

But put that larger point aside here and consider what is going on in this example. Most of us would at least normally think that free speech notions carry with them more concern for and protection of speaking the truth than the non-truth. And when it's a straight out contest between (a) saying what is true and (b) blocking it or repressing it or inhibiting it because it is offensive to some group or subgroup, then shunning (a) in favour of (b) poses threats or challenges to the long-term health of democratic decision-making.

Look at it this way. What person X can say or cannot say – when perceived offensiveness can at least sometimes trump truth – becomes hostage to how thin-skinned person Y happens to be. If Y takes offence easily, or has little sense of humour, or feels her deep-seated convictions ought never to be questioned, then X's scope to speak is more circumscribed than if person Y had a thicker skin or the semblance of a sense of humour.

This is true whatever the source or genealogy of that limit on speech. So we need to be careful; and we need to be careful even though we are well aware there is widespread disagreement in society about where, precisely, to strike this balance between free speech concerns and all those other concerns that seek to put limits on speech.

The rise of such limits growing out of "I am offended" – type concerns, and seen most clearly in hate-speech laws, therefore worries me. I think it poses long-term challenges to democracy. It may further diminish the scope for majoritarian, democratic decision-making, most obviously by making it abundantly clear to everyone that if they can present themselves as thin-skinned, offended victims (whether they really feel that way or not), they might win a political battle they would otherwise lose in the give-and-take of electoral politics.

Moreover, this more New Age hate-speech variant goes hand-in-hand with older, longer-standing speech-stifling tactics. Staying in Canada, think here of the 2010 example of American broadcaster Ann Coulter being intimidated away from speaking at the University of Ottawa – by crowds, by a speech-stifling anticipatory letter from the university provost (one we subsequently learned he was instructed to write by the university president), and by the university's unwillingness to safeguard the venue.[9]

So, yes, next to no one thinks free speech is an absolute good. And, yes, all of us disagree about how much weight to give it against the demands of other values and considerations. Nevertheless, relatively recent attacks on free speech in the name of hate speech eradication, as well as related attempts just to cabin the scope for speech and discussion on contentious and heated social issues, pose a threat to democracy. Long term it does, at any rate. Or such is my first speculation about possible future challenges to democratic decision-making.

My next pre-emptive worry can be boiled down to what I will label "intolerant world views." Leave aside the connections between this category and attacks on free speech for the moment, and remember that we are talking in the realm of speculation. And in that realm it is difficult to see how majoritarianism meshes terribly well with any "I'm doing God's work while you are the spawn of the devil, damned for your wickedness" mindset.

The former, majoritarianism, is a procedure for overcoming social disagreement where all sides believe they are correct, be it morally correct, politically correct, tactically correct, or any other criteria of correctness. At least in part, therefore, any commitment to democracy is a commitment to process and procedure and reciprocity and secondarily or indirectly to the possibility of convincing others (and so, because of the reciprocal nature of the commitment, to being convinced yourself) and to counting all voters' views equally. No matter how you slice it, in other words, any attachment to democracy brings with it a bit of humble pie. And some tolerance for the views of others, if only in the form of a willingness to abide by the majority view until an effective political campaign can be waged to make your currently minority position the majority one.

The latter mindset, which I am loosely labelling the "intolerant world view," carries with it a thorough conviction in the rightness of its own views. More to the point, it is a conviction that puts considerably less weight on *how* decisions are made in society and hence less weight on the procedural legitimacy that flows from the humbleness, tolerance and counting of all people's views equally to start that I mentioned above. What matters under this mindset, what overwhelmingly matters, is therefore living in a society that functions in accord with God's precepts or in a way that does not oppress the proletariat and siphon off the surplus value of its labour or pick your favourite higher good. The point is that beyond a certain level of intolerance for the views and practices of others and democracy does not function well.

My second speculative worry centres on that. And here it simply does not matter from where the threat of that intolerance might be coming. It could be a Samuel Huntington–type *Clash of Civilizations and the Remaking of World Order*,[10] with the main blocks of Western, Muslim, and Confucian civilization facing off and the demographically expanding Islam creating most of that intolerance for democracies. On this scenario you talk demographics, comparative fertility rates, whether the West's universalist claims are pretense or plausible, which may for some (not me) lead on to the occasional discussion of whether all Huntington's blocks – not just the West, but the Muslim, Confucian, Hindu, and other ones – will one day converge on some version or other of liberal capitalist democracy, in line with *The End of History* – type claims of Francis Fukuyama.[11] You might go further on this Huntington scenario, of course, and point to the extremely malign effects of massive Saudi Arabian funding of their Wahhabi brand of radical, fundamentalist Islam, a 2003 CIA report estimating the amounts worldwide to be at least $2 billion a year over thirty-plus years, which if correct buys a fair amount of intolerance.

That's one potential source of the intolerance that could in future pose a threat or challenge to democracy. Radical Islam pretty clearly has trouble co-existing with majoritarian democracy, and does so even where the vast majority of a nation are practising Muslims.

But notice that it could be any intolerant religious denomination or outlook that increases its share of the population over time that provides the source of the worry here. Or at least any worldview that insists on its core precepts being non-negotiable and outside the hurly-burly of democratic negotiation and compromise.

It doesn't really matter for my present purposes from where any future source of intolerance might come. Some anticipated or predicted sources will look more likely to come to pass than others, but all such prognostications are based on extrapolations of current trends, things such as birth rates and immigration rates. And these can change in the future. Today's extrapolation can look pretty silly twenty years hence, or perhaps it can look amazingly prescient. No one knows for sure.

On top of that, intolerance is not just a fault of some of those religiously inclined. Lots of secular atheists can be, and are, every bit as intolerant as your Kansan creationist (though it might also be the case that only hard-core religious intolerance is likely to produce sufficient numbers of people prepared to die, and to kill, for their beliefs – and so intimidate many others from openly debating with them). That said, in a book such as this lamenting the decline in democracy and hoping to spur a reversal in that decline, there is no need to delve into what is the most likely cause or source of future intolerance. In these speculations I simply need to raise the issue. Intolerant world views, beyond a certain level of intolerance at any rate, pose a challenge or threat to society's commitment to letting the numbers count as a procedure to resolve, until the next election, deep-seated social policy disagreements. And hence this is my second speculative worry about possible future challenges threatening more democratic decline.

Having said that, I ought to take a few paragraphs to make clear to readers that tolerance and intolerance are relative concepts. If you think of good qualities the way the Ancient Greeks did, as virtues, then you will see that you can have too much of a good thing just as you can have too little of it. Bravery is a virtue, and highly desirable. But too much of it and it dissolves into recklessness or foolhardiness. One aims for the golden mean, enough bravery but not too much.

The same goes for tolerance. Those who have it possess a desirable, commendable trait or quality. But tolerating everything, even outlooks or worldviews or cultural predispositions bent on destroying your own, is a sort of tolerance that is indistinguishable from weakness. This unrelenting and unbounded sort of tolerance is not desirable. It is to be resisted.

So my worry here about intolerant world views that might pose a threat to democracy must be understood in that context, with that caveat. There is an inescapable element of needed reciprocity to tolerance; live-and-let-live is not a sensible or praiseworthy attitude to take to those who, on their part, do not seek to let you live. And the same goes for those fundamentally opposed to democracy. Tolerating that is weakness, not any quality worth praising.

My third worry or speculative concern relates to the trend toward ever greater internationalization. I worry this will further diminish democracy, or buttress the current trend in that direction. First off, as I have suggested already, democratic decision-making doesn't work well at the supranational level. It works best within the nation-state. At the supranational level you might have a club for democracies (as in the EU), or a talking shop for all nations (as in the UN). The former gives countries votes and it gives individual voters a vote to elect people to a parliament or legislature. But that legislature is far from full-blooded (it can't even initiate laws), while voters do not get to elect a government. The latter, of course, is worse. There is no individual voter input into the UN or any of its agencies or offshoots or into who is chosen to lead or staff any of them. At best it is voting by nation-states with a veto system in the hands of what were the great powers after World War II. This UN system may well be less bad than most plausible alternatives, but it is without doubt democratically deficient, and that is putting the point mildly.

By the trend toward ever greater internationalization I mean the expanding role and decision-making power of UN bodies and other supranational groupings; I mean not just the proliferating number of treaties and conventions that are signed and entered into, but the way judges in democratic countries like our five use them to influence the interpretation of statutes and constitutions, and do so even where (as in all our countries save the United States) the treaties have been agreed to solely by the executive branch and are understood not to be part of domestic law, while in the United States unratified treaties are on occasion referred to as an aid to interpreting the constitution; and I mean the approval and cheerleading for this process that comes from big chunks of the professoriat in universities, the opinion piece writers in newspapers, top civil servants, in short big sections of the elite or intelligentsia or even sometimes the mainstream media, who place too little faith and confidence in democracy and in the opinions of their fellow citizens. One has the sense many of these proponents of souped-up internationalization are considerably more comfortable with the views of their counterparts from abroad and those working with international organizations than with those of their fellow countrymen.

That trend is a third ground for worry as far as future democratic decline goes. And to see how difficult it appears to be to resist, consider the backbone that has disappeared from the Conservative Party in the United Kingdom. That party came just short of outright victory in the 2010 election but managed to form government with the Liberal Democrat Party as the major component of a coalition government. And what has this self-confessedly EU skeptical party agreed to since that election? Having ruled out the promised referendum on the Lisbon Treaty, it voted in favour of a new EU diplomatic service, despite its pre-election manifesto explicitly committing the party to oppose this. It signed up to the EU Investigation Order (where prosecutors from other EU countries can demand and get a British citizen's bank details or DNA with few if any safeguards and little recourse). The Conservative Party has even agreed, albeit with negotiated limits built in, to let the City of London's financial services be regulated by Brussels.

All in all, if that's the Conservative Party's backbone it's the backbone of an invertebrate. And Prime Minister Cameron's vague pledge, and then support for a Private Member's Bill, to hold an in-out (of the EU) referendum in 2017 – to give voters a say some four years down the road on a yet to be wholly locked-in question and a say that is still subject to what happens at the intervening election most probably to be held in 2015 – does not go all that far in growing some democratic spine. I know the UK faces special difficulties resisting internationalization because of its membership in the EU. But the erosion of democratic decision-making there is a big worry.

My fourth challenge for democracy, the last I will list here, I will call mass immigration of the illegal or unauthorized variety. The dangers here are fairly obvious. First off, illegal immigrants usually cannot vote. They aren't part of the numbers that will count; they can't have a say, a vote, be it with the majority or with the minority, just no say at all. This is wholly understandable when people arrive and stay illegally. But it is not good for democracy.

It may not be sustainable either, as the children of illegal immigrants (or at least those born in the new country) will get to vote. And that provides incentives to governments that expect to win the bulk of these people's votes to welcome more of them into the country, either illegally or by loosening the rules to accept them legally.

However it might be devised, if you can relatively swiftly alter who gets a vote by importing 3 million people into Britain in the Blair/Brown years, or five times that many into the United States over the same time, then you move some way toward changing democracy from "electors choosing their government" to "governments choosing their electors." In the language of sticks and carrots, you provide democratically elected governments with an incentive to try to boost the numbers of those likely to side with it, rather than the opposition. This is not unlike the temptation to gerrymander electoral boundaries. In fact it seems every bit as corrosive of democracy as that temptation. When the scale is large enough, it can seem to be an indirect undermining of the nation-state, the level at which democracy works best, as we have seen.

I have no easy suggestion to make that might alleviate this fourth threat; I'm not even fully convinced it has to be a threat. But it probably is. Some immigration in and out of our five countries is clearly a good thing, a net benefit. Illegal immigration, though, looks to be far less of a benefit, however exceedingly tough to stop. Perhaps it's impossible to stop. Then there are the refugees, some political and some only economic but the two sorts near on indistinguishable after the latter have received some basic coaching about what to say to immigration officers.

Certainly big numbers of immigrants have been absorbed in the past by all five of our countries. And that is grounds for optimism. But the changing nature of our economies, and concerns about taking disappearing jobs, point to pessimism. So does an enervated willingness on the part of host countries to insist on assimilation and adoption of core values, including a core commitment to democracy. The same goes more broadly for a lack of willingness, or an apparent one anyway, to defend our democratic set-up as the best one going. Cultural relativism writ large is self-defeating; it's for losers; and it ignores the facts on the ground, namely that only certain civilizations have fostered the scientific know-how that has given us jet planes, antibiotics, a doubling of expected life spans in little over a century, safe and certain contraception, and on and on, while also improving massively the relative position of women. As British philosopher Simon Blackburn puts it:

> There may be rhetoric about the socially constructed nature of Western science, but wherever it matters, there is no alternative. There are no specifically Hindu or Taoist designs for mobile phones, faxes or televisions. There are no satellites based on feminist alternatives to quantum theory. Even that great public skeptic about the value of science, Prince Charles, never flies a helicopter burning homeopathically diluted petrol, that is, water with only a memory of benzene molecules, maintained by a schedule derived from reading tea leaves, and navigated by a crystal ball.[12]

To sum up, I am disposed to be optimistic about the effects of immigration on democracy in our five countries, or to be more accurate of legal immigration. But however disposed or pre-disposed in that direction, I do have my doubts and worries as regards the illegal or not-playing-by-the-rules variety.

I leave it to the reader to add to this short list of challenges to democracy. We need to articulate them not because we predict they will prevail against democracy or inevitably accentuate decline. We need to voice them to ensure just the opposite, that these threats can be rebuffed.

Concluding Remarks

Let me say it one last time. Democracy is in decline in the Anglo-American rich world. We have not been considering, in this book, the accelerating intrusions into democratic decision-making in Albania, or Russia, or even Italy. No, we have been wholly focused on the United States, the United Kingdom, Canada, Australia, and New Zealand. These are the countries that lie smack dab at the heart of anyone's list of the world's core democracies. They are the oldest ones (with the addition of a Switzerland here or an Iceland there); they are the most stable and continuous; they are the most resilient.

Yet the trend of the last few decades has not been good. Clear and distinct inroads have been made into the scope for majoritarian democratic decision-making in all five of these core countries, whatever the differing foundational or institutional emphases put on it in each.

I have argued that most of the blame for that declining trend in our five countries can be laid at the feet of our top judges (and how they are these days going about their job); at the feet of the expanding reach and purview of international law (be it the treaty-based and explicit sort or the undressed, out-of-view and ratcheting-up customary variety); at the feet of jurisdiction gobbling supranational organizations; at the feet of various elite groups in society (often including lawyers' bodies, top public servants, academics, those in NGOs, the mainstream media, and of course the top judges) who not only wink at this trend but who actively promote it, preferring where possible to ignore, disdain and override the beliefs, values and wishes of the majority of their fellow citizens; and at the feet of some shifting and interconnected combination of all of the above.

Here are the words of the noted legal philosopher and constitutional law scholar, well known in both the UK and the United States, describing the last ever decision by the top UK judges as Law Lords before they became members of their newly established Supreme Court. This was the 2009 *Purdy* decision and Professor John Finnis of Oxford and Notre Dame Universities does not mince his words about it; he argues that all the top UK judges in that case were so wayward that aspects of the decision cannot

> be explained by anything other than an overwhelming concern to demonstrate judicial power by *crushing* a policy of government and Parliament that they viewed with political disfavour ... the judges were abetted by the all but unanimous applause of academic and journalistic commentators enamoured of the "liberal" result ... [Such a trend doing lasting damage to the Rule of Law by encouraging] an attitude of judicial supremacy *over law itself* for the sake of objectives whose pursuit by judges is required neither by the law nor by the constitution, nor by natural human rights.[1]

And though Professor Finnis focuses there on the top UK judges – the ones who have recently also given that country judge-made privacy laws that allow for press-muzzling injunctions and super injunctions and who have made deporting just about anyone, terrorists included and even to places such as Italy, near on impossible (despite control of one's borders being a fundamental aspect of national sovereignty) – the same sort of critique, somewhat lessened in potency, applies to the judges in all of our five countries. Indeed it applies with more potency still to the top European judges who recently ruled[2] that cheaper car insurance for young women than for young men, based as it was wholly on empirical actuarial evidence, was discriminatory, a ruling binding on the UK and its elected legislature. This inane decision provoked one commentator to claim that "the judges are so bewitched by the idea of discrimination that they can't tell the difference between actuaries and Nazis."

But of course it isn't just the judges, however easy it might be to paint the recent 5–4 US Supreme Court decision ordering California to release up to 46,000 prisoners in anti-democratic terms (and I impugn that as someone convinced that the United States incarcerates far too many of its citizens, but who still thinks this is a matter to be fixed through elected politics). It's also a Senate in the United States that refuses to pass a budget; it's an Environmental Protection Agency in that same United States that bypasses the elected Congress; moving north it's the most successful democratic political party of the twentieth century, one elected to office for over two-thirds of those hundred years, Canada's left-of-centre Liberal Party, after being nearly decimated in the 2011 general election, suggesting that the way to win back lost voter support was to amend Canada's Charter of Rights to make it even more all-encompassing by including social and economic rights and thus to inflate still more the power of Canada's unelected judges; and so on and so on and so on ending with democracy's loss of attractiveness to so many in the Western elite.

None of this should be read as apocalyptic, as though democracy in these core countries of ours is on the verge of imminent collapse. If anything my instincts lie more at the optimistic end of the spectrum, the end so well summed up with these words from the Gettysburg Address: "that government of the people, by the people, for the people, shall not perish from the earth."

But that optimism will end up prevailing only where citizens and voters are prepared to stand up against these incremental and piecemeal intrusions, where they have the strength of conviction to withstand the siren song of fatter, more morally pregnant understandings of democracy that downgrade significantly the place given to counting each of us as equal and then letting the numbers count in favour of moral abstractions – perfectionist ones at that – to be given content on a case-by-case basis by our betters, the elites who can supposedly be trusted to uphold these other things that they tell us are necessary adjuncts or components of a "proper" understanding of democracy.

I don't buy that siren song. I've heard it, but it has no appeal to me. You cannot stuff every good thing known to man into your understanding of democracy, and especially when the effect of doing so is to reduce, in practice, the scope for letting the numbers count, majoritarian democracy. Or rather, you cannot do that and keep any strong commitment to the more morally spartan understanding of democracy, the one that does *not* assume that certain self-styled elites have better moral antennae than plumbers, teachers, factory workers or even derivatives traders – as though these elites magically and mysteriously have some sort of pipeline to God on all of society's hotly contested moral and political line-drawing exercises related to such things as euthanasia, abortion, same-sex marriage, illegal immigration, how to balance criminal procedures against the need for public safety, and on and on and on.

Of course if I am right, and clearly I think I am, then that leads us to wonder why democracy and democratic decision-making (in our down-to-earth sense that actually gives each of us a more or less equal vote and say on outcomes) has lost its shine for so many in our five countries. Why has its lustre dimmed for so many internationalists, human rights lawyers, top judges, environmentalists and more? One possible answer, the rather cynical and depressing one, is that these people simply calculate that they can get more of their first-order political and moral preferences satisfied in the courts or via supranational organizations or by appeal to international law than they can by trying to convince their fellow citizens. "I want X, Y, and Z because I believe them to be morally right, or think they lead to the best political outcomes" they calculate to themselves. And they go on to hold those outcomes to be more important than the process of how they are reached and achieved, however elitist and top-down the process may be.

However, people who make that calculation have great difficulties in saying so openly, not least because everyone thinks his or her views are the morally right ones and the ones that will lead to best outcomes. So you can hardly come out and say, at least not too often, that your opponents are stupid, dumb and in need of re-education but that you yourself are wisdom and enlightenment incarnate. In other words it's hard to be against democracy and democratic decision-making in the full light of day, remembering that we're talking about the United States, the UK, Canada, Australia, and New Zealand.

This cynical attempt to do an end run around the views of your fellow citizens is only remotely palatable when kept disguised and secret and out of view. This tactic works better by keeping people's gazes focused up on the Olympian heights of moral abstractions and as far from possible on who is making these decisions you happen to think preferable, and how they are doing it. Otherwise people will be inclined to think their own moral and political views are as good as the next guy's, and expect them to be treated as such. Otherwise they'll insist on decision-making by letting the numbers count, the greater satisfying of *your* particular druthers through the courts or by appeal to international law and supranational organizations be damned.

I am much of that way of thinking. If this book goes any distance at all in removing some of the obfuscations that have contributed to the decline in democracy in our five countries, I will be more than happy.

Another possible answer to why my sort of democratic decision-making has lost its lustre for some is that events are seen simply to have gotten away from everyone. The point here isn't as above that you generally like the answers coming from the courts, the EU, international law and the various second-tier UN agencies more than you like what democratic politics throws up. No, the answer here that tries to account for democracy's lack of lustre for some relates more to despair than cynicism. Here reside the people who simply feel that nothing much can be done to win back recently lost room for democratic decision-making. So it's all about managing democratic decline, as it were, even though one would prefer for there not to be that decline.

Think here of the erstwhile defender of democracy in Britain who looks and sees what the Tony Blair/Gordon Brown government's creation of a statutory bill of rights Human Rights Act linked to the European Convention of Human Rights has done. This person sees that it has led to the UK judges virtually halting deportations of dangerous foreign nationals. It has led to active combat soldiers being required to apply convention rulings to the way they operate at war. It has fostered an explosion in the compensation culture, with costs of around £25 billion to date and about £7 billion per year as things stand at present. It has increased, remarkably, the percentage of cases the UK loses in the Strasbourg Court, which is now over 75 per cent overall. It has resulted in costs of compliance with convention rulings from there of over £2 billion per year, and total costs to date of over £17 billion.[3] And then when that same European Strasbourg Court decides to overrule the UK Parliament on when convicted and serving prisoners can and cannot vote – as it did in late 2010 – this person simply throws up his hands and gives up. This erstwhile defender of democracy decides that fighting this might align him with too many people whose views he finds distasteful. Or he thinks the costs of yet another incremental incursion won't be so terribly, terribly awful, not when put in the context of the earlier incursions. Or he just hasn't got the stomach for the fight.

So he paints the ruling from the Strasbourg Court as not so terribly bad and tries to minimize it.

Now we can all be cheered by the fact that in real life the elected members of the UK Parliament in early 2011 chose in this instance to stand up to the European Court and voted to ignore its ruling. What the David Cameron coalition government will in fact do now, in the light of that parliamentary display of what might be described as "backbone," is unclear, but it would be rash to get too optimistic. Let us simply say that this is one of the rare hopeful signs coming out of the UK of late.

Of course we can speculate on other causes of democracy's lost lustre too. The default genuflecting before cultural relativism might play a role. So too might the widespread tendency in the schools, when educating the next generation, to adopt a sort of self-loathing outlook that applies a far harsher (and bizarrely ahistorical) standard of judgment to our past actions than to those of other cultures and nations. Or perhaps the examples of dysfunctional democratic set-ups such as Belgium and Italy don't help. Or maybe people these days, across a range of issues, are just less motivated and keen to fight for their freedoms and their democracy than in the past. Whatever the causes for the dimming of democracy's lustre, and most particularly among the sort of left-wing activists who a generation or two before were the ones most active in promoting it but now are not, the fact remains that democracy and democratic decision-making has lost its shine for too many in our five countries. And that is a cause for concern and something to be lamented.

I said I was ultimately optimistic about the place of democracy in our five countries, though more so in some than others. I can say that and still wonder what sort of signal this decline in the core democratic countries on earth sends to more marginal or penumbral democratic countries.

Here's what it boils down to. No one living in a democracy can expect to be on the winning side of every social policy argument. And that's true even when the argument is recast in the language of rights. And even again when you care really, really deeply about the outcome. All of us care about rights. All of us think our beliefs, sentiments and views are the right ones. But when the default and immediate position of those who lose in the court of public opinion and majoritarian voting is to head straight off to the courts or international agencies – even when such routes were formerly considered for this or that dispute to be unavailable – then you have a problem. It does not amount to a tyranny of the majority every time one side wins a vote and the other loses. That, to the contrary, is what lies at the heart of democracy.

One's remedy when she finds herself on the wrong side of an issue about which she feels strongly is to spend a few Saturdays working and campaigning for candidates and political parties that will seek to persuade the majority to change its mind and then to reverse the decision. Losing a vote is not tyranny. (I say nothing about how, throughout history, the tyranny of the minority has been a much more potent and deadly sort of tyranny than the sort practised by the majority. Majorities still have a lot to learn about tyranny from minorities.)

That's the message we need to make loud and clear. Sometimes you can be right on substance and nevertheless lose and yet the procedure that produced that outcome can be the right one, the best one, the one that ought to prevail.

Nothing in any of these concluding remarks should be taken to suggest I think of democracy in perfectionist terms. I do not. No, I see it in very Churchillian terms as the worst form of government going, except for every other one so far tried. Mine is very much a least-bad endorsement, not a "this is wonderful and perfect" endorsement. We can all sit around poking holes in the electoral arrangements here or there – gerrymandering, the voting system, too much reliance on referenda (or too little), upper houses that aren't elected, upper houses that favour voters in small states over big ones, lack of primaries, what have you. But none of that makes any alternative such as rule by judges or by the Harvard Common Room or by London or East Coast elites or by apolitical civil servants preferable.

Letting-the-numbers-count majoritarian democracy delivers the best consequences, on average, over time. The recent decline in that sort of democracy in five of the oldest and most stable democracies in the world needs to be stopped and then reversed. Starting now.

Suggested Further Reading

Alexander, Larry. *Constitutionalism: Philosophical Foundations.* Cambridge, UK: Cambridge University Press, 1998.

Aroney, Nicholas. *The Constitution of a Federal Commonwealth: The Making and Meaning of the Australian Constitution.* Cambridge, UK: Cambridge University Press, 2009.

Campbell, Tom, et al. eds. *The Legal Protection of Human Rights: Sceptical Essays.* Oxford, UK: Oxford University Press, 2011.

Ekins, Richard, ed. *Modern Challenges to the Rule of Law.* Wellington, NZ: Lexis Nexis, 2011, especially the chapter "Invoking the Principle of Legality against the Rule of Law" by John Finnis, p. 129.

Goldsworthy, Jeffery. *Parliamentary Sovereignty.* Cambridge, UK: Cambridge University Press, 2010.

Hirschl, Ran. *Towards Juristocracy: The Origins and Consequences of the New Constitutionalism.* Cambridge, MA: Harvard University Press, 2004.

Hix, Simon. *What's Wrong with the European Union and How to Fix It.* Cambridge, UK: Polity, 2008.

Huscroft, Grant and Bradley Miller, eds. *The Challenge of Originalism: Theories of Constitutional Interpretation.* New York: Cambridge University Press, 2011.

– and Ian Brodie, eds. *Constitutionalism in the Charter Era.* Markham, ON: LexisNexis, 2004, especially the chapter "Romancing the Constitution: Interpretation as Invention" by Antonin Scalia, p. 337.

McGinnis, John et al., "The Patterns and Implications of Political Contributions by Elite Law School Faculty." *Georgia Law Journal* 93 (2005): 1167.

– and Ilya Somin. "Should International Law Be Part of Our Law?" *Stanford Law Review* 59 (2007): 1175.

Posner, Richard. "No Thanks, We Already Have Our Own Laws." *Legal Affairs*. (July/August 2004).

– *Frontiers of Legal Theory*. Cambridge, MA: Harvard University Press, 2001.

Rodger, Lord Earlsferry. "Judges and Academic Lawyers in the United Kingdom." *University of Queensland Law Journal* 29 (2010): 29.

Rotherham, Lee. *Britain and the ECHR*. London: TaxPayers' Alliance, 2011.

Scalia, Antonin. *A Matter of Interpretation*. Princeton, NJ: Princeton University Press, 1997.

Smith, Steven D. *Law's Quandary*. Cambridge, MA: Harvard University Press, 2004.

Sowell, Thomas. *The Vision of the Anointed: Self-Congratulation as a Basis for Social Policy*. New York: Basic Books, 1995.

Steyn, Mark. *America Alone: The End of the World as We Know It*. Washington, DC: Regnery, 2006.

Sumption, Jonathan. "Judicial and Political Decision-Making: The Uncertain Boundary." The F.A. Mann 2011 Lecture in *Judicial Review* 16 (2011): 301.

Tushnet, Mark. "Academics as Lawmakers?" *University of Queensland Law Journal* 29 (2010): 19.

Waldron, Jeremy. *Law and Disagreement*. Oxford, UK: Oxford University Press, 1999.

Notes

PREFACE

1 For example, the Nobel Prize–winning economist Amartya Sen. See "Democracy as a Universal Value," *Journal of Democracy* 10 (1999): 8. See also Ronald Dworkin, *A Bill of Rights for Britain* (London: Chatto & Windus, 1990), 43: "[d]emocracy is not the same thing as majority rule, and that in a real democracy liberty and minorities have legal protection."
2 In *Re Marriage Cases* (2008) 183 P. 3d 384; 43 Cal. 4th 757 (Cal. Sup. Ct.).
3 Meaning same-sex marriages that had taken place between the time the California Supreme Court struck down the statute and the day Proposition 8 was adopted and changed the state constitution were held valid.
4 Of the US states that allow same-sex marriage, only a distinct minority of these, including New York, have legislated for same-sex marriage, the rest having it brought into being by the unelected judges. As for referenda attempts to constitutionally ban same-sex marriage at the state level, these sometimes succeed and sometimes fail, though attempts to mandate it by referendum where it is put directly to the voters in a popular vote have all been defeated.

INTRODUCTION

1 In a speech in the House of Commons on November 11, 1947, Winston Churchill said: "No one pretends that democracy is perfect or all-wise. Indeed, it has been said that democracy is the worst form of government except all those other forms that have been tried from time to time."

COUNTRIES IN DECLINE

1. See Nick Aroney, *The Constitution of a Federal Commonwealth: The Making and Meaning of the Australian Constitution* (Cambridge: Cambridge University Press, 2009).
2. The French Declaration of the Rights of Man is slightly older than the American Bill of Rights, though the now states of Virginia, Pennsylvania, Maryland, North Carolina, Vermont, Massachusetts, and New Hampshire have older bills of rights than either of these countries.
3. See John McGinnis's study on donations by elite international law professors in the United States favouring Democrats over Republicans by more than five to one. John McGinnis et al., "The Patterns and Implications of Political Contributions by Elite Law School Faculty," *Georgia Law Journal* 93 (2005): 1167.
4. This basic position was slightly altered in the United Kingdom by the Constitutional Reform and Governance Act 2010, sections 20–23, allowing Parliament to pass a resolution *not* to ratify a treaty. However, under section 22 any minister may opt not to refer a treaty to Parliament, and so to bypass this new "ask Parliament" regime entirely, and without any recourse by the legislature. In addition, the upper house has no real "do not ratify" power under this statute. And section 23 exempts certain categories of treaty entirely. So on balance I believe that my claim in the main text remains largely correct for the United Kingdom too.
5. An interesting question is whether this Senate rule could be altered by a straight-up 51–49, or majority, vote. Current Senate rules say no, that changes to the rules need a two-thirds majority. But a nineteenth-century Supreme Court precedent (*US v. Ballin*) says a simple majority vote would suffice. Note, too, that these days the talking aspect of this "talking the bill out" tactic is not actually required.
6. The twenty least-populated states account for about 11 per cent of the US population. See *The Economist*, February 20, 2010.
7. The three victorious US presidents who nevertheless obtained fewer votes than someone else were Rutherford Hayes (1876), Benjamin Harrison (1888), and George W. Bush (2000).
8. There have been twenty-seven successful amendments to the US Constitution: the first ten in 1791 (together known as the Bill of Rights) and the last one in 1992.
9. So with Australia currently having six states, to succeed a majority of voters in four of the states must pass the amendment, as well as a majority

nationwide. This is a considerably easier amending hurdle, procedurally speaking, than the American one.

10 And as I explained, only the American one was justiciable or able to be used in court to have judges strike down statutes passed by the legislature. The French one became justiciable in this sense only in 2008.

11 Other democratic countries that are generally classed as unitary systems include France, Japan, and Britain, though recent reforms in the last of these have created a quasi- (or less kindly, a pseudo-) federal system. In its early colonial days New Zealand had provinces, but they did not survive the transition to self-government.

12 New Zealand has never lost a WTO case, and its farmers receive virtually no subsidies or protection at all.

13 MMP works by giving each voter two votes. Just over half of all legislators are chosen from single member constituencies or districts in the former FPP way, and each voter gets one vote for that. The second vote, and the more important one, is for the voter's preferred party. Just under half of all legislators are chosen from lists prepared by the parties. You get proportionality – meaning the percentage of a party's vote on this second prong more or less reflects the percentage of representatives it will get in the legislature – because after the district or constituency winners are determined, you simply use the lists of party-supplied names to top-up each party's results. So if party A wins ten districts or constituencies in a one-hundred-member legislature, and it wins 20 per cent of the party vote, then it receives a further ten people, taken directly off the party's list, as top-up members of the legislature. In New Zealand these are known as list MPs.

14 And all ten provinces in Canada have simple, undisguised unicameral legislatures, with no pretense even of an upper house.

15 American readers can think of the prerogative power as the left-over bits of power that at one time were in the hands of the monarch and have not been taken or claimed by Parliament, though these powers are now in substance all exercised by the elected prime minister and Cabinet. Prerogative power, then, is executive power which can be exercised over matters (for example, declaring war) without the need for any statute being passed through the legislature.

16 Early on after the Charter of Rights was adopted the French-speaking province of Quebec's legislature invoked section 33 a number of times, especially on language matters. A couple of other provinces invoked it early on too. But even provincial use of section 33 has long ago died out.

And as noted in the main text, section 33 has never been invoked federally, not one single time ever.
17 One such is the Oxford University legal academic Aileen Kavanagh. See, for example, her *Constitutional Review under the UK Human Rights Act* (Cambridge: Cambridge University Press, 2009).
18 See, for example, Thomas Pogge, "Creating Supranational Institutions Democratically: Reflections on the European Union's 'Democratic Deficit,'" in *Democracy in the European Union,* eds., Andreas Follesdal and Peter Koslowski (Berlin: Springer, 1998), 160.
19 See *Australian Capital Television Pty Ltd v. Commonwealth* (No 2) (1992) 177 CLR 106.
20 See Graeme Orr, *The Law of Politics* (Leichhardt, AU: The Federation Press, 2010), chap. 3.

CAUSES OF DECLINE

1 New Zealand and the UK being unitary states.
2 Justice Antonin Scalia, "Romancing the Constitution: Interpretation as Invention," in *Constitutionalism in the Charter Era,* eds. Ian Ross Brodie and Grant Huscroft (Markham, ON: LexisNexis, 2004), 337.
3 A digression here might take the interested reader into how a theory of interpretation (i.e., how best to give meaning to the words before you) differs from a theory of when judicial disobedience is warranted (of when judges who know the law's words mean X are justified in announcing they mean not-X). Certainly I would say that circumstances can be imagined when the right thing to do as a judge is to achieve outcome not-X, even though that involves dishonest interpretation. We need not even imagine this but simply put ourselves in the shoes of apartheid-era South African judges to see this is at least a possibility. But anyone who calculated the best likely consequences pointed in favour of this sort of judicial lying would have to admit the judge doing so was not interpreting. It may be justified – even in a democracy, though my view is that in a well-functioning democracy it will be exceptionally rare that it is justified as opposed to resigning one's judgeship – but it is not interpretation.
4 410 US 113 (1973).
5 *Baigent's Case* [1994] 3 NZLR 667.
6 Here are three of the important ones: ACTV (1992) 177 CLR 106; Nationwide News (1992) 177 CLR 1; and Lange (1997) 189 CLR 520.
7 *Ghaidan v. Godin-Mendoza* [2004] 3 All ER 411; 2 AC 557.

8   Start with these, for a taste: *Sauve #1* [1993] 2 SCR 438 and *Sauve #2* [2002] 3 SCR 519 (on prisoner voting); *Singh* [1985] 1 SCR 177 (on the entitlements of refugee claimants); *Harper* [2004] 1 SCR 827 and *Libman* [1997] 3 SCR 569 (on what campaign finance rules are acceptable); *Halpern* [2003] OJ 2268 (ruling that confining marriage to opposite-sex couples was unconstitutional and hence judicially legislating for same-sex marriage); and *Morgentaler* [1988] 1 SCR 30 (striking down compromise abortion legislation thereby leaving the field wide open and unrestricted).
9   See Jeffrey Goldsworthy, "Parliamentary Sovereignty and Statutary Interpretation," chap. 9 in *Parliamentary Sovereignty* (Cambridge: Cambridge University Press, 2010).
10 We might like, here, to distinguish appeals to other countries once part of the same overarching empire or commonwealth, such as Canada, Australia, New Zealand, and the UK, from appeals to foreign law in other senses. Or perhaps not.
11 See James Allan, Grant Huscroft, and Nessa Lynch, "The Citation of Overseas Authority in Rights Litigation in New Zealand: How Much Bark? How Much Bite?," *Otago Law Review* 11 (2007): 433.
12 See *Knight v. Florida* 528 U.S. 990 (1999).
13 See the poll conducted by the University of Maryland and World Public Opinion in 2007 conducted in Egypt, Morocco, Pakistan, and Indonesia.
14 543 US 551, 567 (Kennedy J).
15 560 US (2010) (Kennedy J).
16 See, for instance, Tom Campbell, K.D. Ewing, and Adam Tomkins, eds., *The Legal Protection of Human Rights: Sceptical Essays* (Oxford: Oxford University Press, 2011).
17 In the early Canadian Charter of Rights case of *Hunter v. Southam Inc* [1984] 2 S.C.R. 145 (Can.) then Justice Dickson, at p 155, said: "The task of expounding a constitution is crucially different from that of construing a statute ... Once enacted, its provisions cannot easily be repealed or amended. It must, therefore, be capable of growth and development over time to meet new social, political and historical realities often unimagined by its framers. The judiciary is the guardian of the constitution and must, in interpreting its provisions, bear these considerations in mind" (Italics mine).
18 See *Sauve v. Canada* (Chief Electoral Officer) [2002] 3 SCR 519 at paragraph [41].
19 New Zealand Bill of Rights Act 1990 pt 1 s 4.
20 See *Ministry of Transport v. Noort* [1992] 3 NZLR 260 at 270–1: "The [Bill of Rights] Act requires development of the law where necessary. Such

21 *Ghaidan v. Godin-Mendoza* [2004] 2 AC 557, 571–2.
22 Ibid. at [111] (Lord Rodger).
23 *Jackson v. Attorney General* [2006] 1 AC 262 at [102] (Lord Steyn).
24 See Kavanagh, *Constitutional Review under the UK Human Rights Act*.
25 And for what it's worth, the inroads into the ideals undergirding the notion of the rule of law have been worse still – even more pronounced – in the UK than in New Zealand.
26 For those interested in minutiae, Australian judges do have federalism power – with a written, federal constitution along American lines they have final, authoritative power to decide if some legislative enactment lies within the aegis of the federal legislature or of those of the states. In that context Australian judges can strike down and invalidate democratically enacted laws. But this is umpiring or choosing between different elected legislatures. It is not announcing that no elected legislature can do it because, in the judges' view (or view of a majority of them) it conflicts with what some moral abstraction (enunciated in the language of rights and probably interpreted as a "living" thing whose reach varies over time – possibly due to the "empathy" a particular judge brings to the task) requires.
27 If it were necessary to win the approval of the lower house that would be guaranteed in a Westminster system where the government – by definition – retains the confidence of the lower house, meaning it wins all important votes in that chamber.
28 See "Selection Process Overview," Judicial Appointments Commission, http://jac.judiciary.gov.uk/selection-process/352.htm.
29 See Jeremy Bentham, *An Introduction to the Principles of Morals and Legislation,* eds. J.H. Burns and H.L.A. Hart (1780; reprint London: Methuen, 1982).
30 See Gerald Postema, *Bentham and the Common Law Tradition* (Oxford: Oxford University Press, 1989).
31 Office of the UN High Commissioner for Human Rights, Committee on the Rights of the Child, General Comment No. 8: "The right of the child to protection from corporal punishment and other cruel or degrading forms of punishment," 42nd sess, UN Doc CRC/C/GC/8 (March 2, 2007) http://www2.ohchr.org/english/bodies/crc/comments.htm.
32 Four to three in the High Court of Australia case of *Al-Kateb v. Goodwin* (2004) 208 ALR 124; 78 ALJR 1099.

33 *Roper v. Simmons*, 543 U.S. 551 (2005).
34 Associate Justice Ruth Ginsburg, "A Decent Respect to the Opinions of [Human]kind: The Value of a Comparative Perspective in Constitutional Adjudication," keynote address at the Annual Meeting of the American Society of International Law, April 2005.
35 Associate Justice Sandra Day O'Connor, keynote address at the Annual Meeting of the American Society of International Law, 2002.
36 See Jeremy Waldron, *Law and Disagreement* (Oxford: Oxford University Press, 1999).
37 Lord Rodger of Earlsferry, "Judges and Academics in the United Kingdom," *University of Queensland Law Journal* 29 no. 29 (2010): 39.
38 Mark Tushnet, "Academics as Law-Makers?," *University of Queensland Law Journal* 29 no.19 (2010): 20.
39 See John McGinnis, "The Patterns and Implications of Political Contributions by Elite Law School Faculty." *Georgetown Law Journal* 93 (2005): 1,167–82.
40 Tushnet, "Academics as Law-Makers?," 20.
41 Louis Sohn, "Sources of International Law," *Georgia Journal of International and Comparative Law* 25 (1996): 399.
42 See Spencer Zifcak, "Reforming the United Nations: The North-South Impasse," chap. 9 in *United Nations Reform: Heading North or South?* (Oxford: Routledge, 2009).
43 McGinnis and Ilya Somin, "Should International Law Be Part of Our Law?," *Stanford Law Review* 59 (2007): 1,175–99.
44 Ibid., 1200.
45 See Peter Mair and Jacques Thomassen, "Political Representation and Government in the European Union," *Journal of European Public Policy* 17 no.1 (2010): 20–35.
46 See Simon Hix, *What's Wrong with the European Union and How to Fix It* (Cambridge, UK: Polity, 2008).
47 *R v. Secretary of State for Transport*, ex p. Factortame Ltd [1989] 2 All ER 692; *R v. Secretary of State for Transport ex p. Factortame Ltd (Interim Relief Order)* [1990] UKHL 7.
48 See Zifcak, 67–74.
49 For more detail on the WTO see Raj Bhala, *International Trade Law: Interdisciplinary Theory and Practice*, 3rd ed. (Newark, NJ: LexisNexis, 2008).
50 *RJR-MacDonald Inc v. Canada* (Attorney General) [1995] 3 SCR 199.
51 *Halpern v. Canada* (2003) 225 D.L.R. (4th) 529 (Ontario Court of Appeal). Legislation was passed after this Halpern decision extending the

result nationally, but only after the receipt of the advisory opinion of the Supreme Court of Canada in Reference re: Same-Sex Marriage [2004] 3 S.C.R. 698.
52 *Singh v. Minister of Employment and Immigration* [1985] 1 S.C.R. 177.
53 *R. v. Morgentaler* [1988] 1 S.C.R. 30.
54 A line of cases beginning with *R. v. Parker* (2000) 188 DLR (4th) 385 (Ontario Court of Appeal), culminating in requirements that the government grow the marijuana in some cases.
55 *Sauve v. Canada* (Attorney General) [2002] 3 S.C.R. 519.
56 Lon Fuller, "The Case of the Speluncean Explorers," *Harvard Law Review* 62 (1949): 616 at pages 636–7 (emphasis mine).
57 Nile Gardiner, "Barack Obama Has Bowed before the UN over Arizona Immigration Law," *The Telegraph* (blog), August 31, 2010, http://blogs.telegraph.co.uk/news/nilegardiner/100051882/barack-obama-bows-before-the-un-over-arizona-immigration-law/.

COMPLICATIONS MASKING DECLINE

1 347 US 483 (1954).

CHALLENGES THREATENING MORE DECLINE

1 The case is *Arizona v. United States*, 567 U.S. ___ (2012), decided by the United States Supreme Court in June, 2012.
2 US Department of State, "Report of the United States of America – Submitted to the UN High Commissioner for Human Rights in Conjunction with the Universal Periodic Review," August 20. 2010, http://www.state.gov/documents/organization/146379.pdf.
3 John Stuart Mill, *On Liberty* (London: J.W. Parker and Son, 1859; New York: The Modern Library, 2002).
4 Ibid., 18–19.
5 I refer to section 13(1) of the Canadian Human Rights Act, which mandates that it is discriminatory to communicate any material "that is *likely* to expose a person to hatred or contempt" (italics mine). (See too the broadly similar section 18C of Australia's Racial Discrimination Act.) Repeal of this Canadian national law, by private member's bill, was passed through the elected House of Commons (lower house) in 2012 and through the unelected upper house Senate in 2013. All that remains is the Royal Assent, which is little more than a formality. So section 13 will be

repealed. However, similar hate-speech provisions still exist in some of the provincial jurisdictions in Canada.

6 See the 1990 Supreme Court of Canada case of CHRC v. Taylor which upheld the constitutional validity of this s.13 and also the 2013 Supreme Court of Canada case of Saskatchewan v. Whatcott, which also upheld the constutional validity of these types of hate-speech provisions.
7 For instance, the UN General Assembly has passed several resolutions urging the adoption of anti-blasphemy laws, in line with the views of the Organization of the Islamic Conference (OIC).
8 See note 6 above.
9 CBC News, "Ann Coulter 'Welcome' at University of Ottawa," March 24, 2010, http://www.cbc.ca/news/canada/ottawa/story/2010/03/24/ottawa-ann-coulter-university.html.
10 Samuel Huntington, *The Clash of Civilizations and the Remaking of World Order* (New York: Simon and Schuster, 1996).
11 Francis Fukuyama, *The End of History and the Last Man* (New York: Free Press, 1992).
12 Simon Blackburn, *Truth: A Guide for the Perplexed* (Allen Lane, 2005), 1.

CONCLUDING REMARKS

1 John Finnis, "Invoking the Principle of Legality against the Rule of Law," in *Modern Challenges to the Rule of Law*, ed. Richard Ekins (Newark, NJ: LexisNexis, 2011), 129–141, commenting in part on the *Purdy* decision [2009] UKHL 45, [2010] 1 AC 345, [2009] 4 All ER 1147 (italics in the original).
2 This is the European Court of Justice case, handed down on March 1, 2011, of *Association Belge des Consommateurs Test-Achats ASBC and Others* (Case C-236/09).
3 All these claims and more can be found in Lee Rotherham, *Britain and the ECHR* (London: TaxPayers Alliance, 2011).

Index

amending a constitution, 16, 35
attack on free speech, 148–53

Bentham, Jeremy, 83–4
bills of rights: Australian exceptionalism, 8, 35, 37, 50, 78, 108; finesse disagreement, 18, 51, 120; historical evolution, 8, 16, 76; how sold to people, 52–3, 55, 66, 75; just buying views of judges, 54, 59, 70; justiciable versions, 16; natural law foundations, 8; nature of such instruments, 17, 64–5, 117; not self-interpreting, 19, 48, 64; section 33 Canadian Charter, 28–9, 66, 72, 123; sorts of questions involved, 17, 34, 48–9, 52, 64–5, 80, 123
Blackburn, Simon, 158
Breyer, Justice Stephen, 93

Churchill, Winston, 4, 166; democracy as worst form except all others, 4
closet aristocracy, 79
common law, 83–5; deficiencies, 84; undemocratic, 84–5
constitutional interpretation, 53–4; before and after vantages, 47–50, 52; debatable calls, 130; democracy enervating effects, 42, 50, 54; legitimacy of text, 46, 48; locking things in, 38, 46, 51–2, 55, 59; non-judge vantage, 55, 66, 126, 130; over-ruling the legislature, 137
constitutional mimicry, 6, 40, 108; Australia and the United States, 34–5
constitutional set-ups, 108, 128–9; checks and balances, 13
Convention on Rights of the Child (CRC), 85–8; article 19, 86–8, 116; relation to spanking, 86–7
conventions, 21. See also treaties
countermajoritarian difficulties, 14, 17–18, 68, 77; over-looked downside, 125
countries with appointed upper houses: UK House of Lords, 7; Canadian Senate, 7, 25–6
cultural relativism, 101–2
customary international law. See undressed international law

Declarations of Incompatibility,
71–2, 142
democracy: morally fat or lean conceptions, 133–6, 148, 162
democratic decision-making, 19,
107; convincing others, 52; effect of international law on, 88, 98; elections as constraints, 22–3; increased judicial power, 82; recent inroads into, 20–1, 64, 68, 72, 137, 144–8, 160
direct democracy, 10

Electoral College, 14–15
elite consensus, 11, 33, 156
European Union (EU): background, 32, 123, 144; Common Agricultural Policy, 111, 113; democratic credentials, 32, 109–10, 112, 130, 145; effect on UK democracy of, 33, 111–13, 130; pros and cons, 33
expanding internationalization, 155–7
expansive and unconstrained interpreting, 3, 29–30, 36–7, 45, 49–50, 57, 60, 65, 130

Factortame, 112
federalism, 15, 21, 146; Canadian vs. US versions, 26–7; competition rationale, 10; quasi-federalism, 32; satisfying more preferences rationale, 10
filibuster, 13–14
Finnis, John, 161
Fukuyama, Francis, 154
Fuller, Lon, 125

gerrymandering, 15–16
Ginsburg, Justice Ruth, 93

human rights activists, 121
Huntington, Samuel, 154

illegal immigration, 157–8
implied rights in Australia, 36–7
International Court of Justice (ICJ), 102–5
international law: dismiss relevance of, 88; in need of debunking, 85; lousy comparative quality, 83
intolerant worldviews, 153–5

judicial appointments, 26–7;
Australian exceptionalism, 78; non-US approach, 76–7; self-selection, 81; UK approach, 78–82; US approach, 73–5, 83
judges: moral input of, 43, 64, 74, 118; power has grown, 82; power of interpreting, 43–4, 63, 68–9, 71; *See also* bills of rights

language of human rights, 110, 117
letting the numbers count, 13, 128–9, 136–7, 153, 162–3
living-constitution interpretation, 59, 62, 64, 117; appeals to foreign law, 55–7; blank cheque, 57, 120; democracy enervating effects, 73; implications, 49, 59

masking democratic decline: Ploy #1, 129–30; Ploy #2, 131–2;
Ploy #3, 132–6; Ploy #4, 137–8;
Ploy #5, 138–40; Ploy #6, 140–1;
Ploy #7, 141–3
McGinnis, John, 105–06
Mill, John Stuart, 148
mixed member proportional, (MMP). *See* voting systems, proportional representation

more constraining interpretive
  approaches, 57–8; floor not ceil-
  ing, 51, 58, 60; originalism,
  58–61; puke-test interpreting, 62

O'Connor, Justice Sandra Day, 93

parliamentary sovereignty, 21, 112

reading-down interpretive mandates, 3, 22, 69–70, 80, 142; *Alice
  in Wonderland* effects, 69–71,
  142; heralds a new legal order, 71
reasonable disagreement, 3, 17–8,
  94, 105, 116, 126, 133–4, 150;
  vs. alleging bad faith, 140–1
Rodger, Lord, 95
Rule of Law, 69–71

Senates, 13; compared to bills of
  rights, 18–19. *See also* countries
  with appointed upper houses
statutory bills of rights: increased
  power of judges, 72–3; NZ version, 22, 66–9; UK Humpty
  Dumpty approach, 45; UK version, 31, 70–2, 144, 164. *See also*
  masking democratic decline; Ploy
  #7; Declarations of
  Incompatibility
Steyn, Mark, 150–1

tolerance, 155
treaties: democratic deficiencies,
  90–1; need for incorporation
  into domestic law, 89; upgrades
  by judges, 90; use of unratified
  ones, 91–5; using to interpret
  domestic law, 12, 90

treaty-making: democratic deficiencies, 40, 90, 96; legislature vs.
  executive, 89; US system, 12;
  in Westminster systems, 89–90
Treaty of Waitangi, 24, 30
Tushnet, Mark, 97–8

undemocratic elites, 121–7; can
  include politicians, 123–5; loss
  of faith in democracy, 122–3
undressed international law,
  96–102; expanding reach, 99,
  104–5; legitimacy, 100–1; passive
  voice, 97; publicists, 97–9, 106;
  two schools, 105–6; undemocratic, 98, 102–7
United Nations (UN), 109, 113–14,
  156
United Nations Commission on
  Human Rights (UNCHR), 114
United Nations Human Rights
  Council (UNHRC), 85, 114–15;
  periodic reviews, 115–17, 147
unwritten constitutions, 7, 20–1

voting systems, 7, 108, 131–2;
  compulsory voting, 38; first past
  the post (FPP), 7, 22–3; parties
  vs. voters, 23; preferential voting,
  7–8, 39; proportional representation (PR), 7, 23

Westminster parliamentary system,
  25
World Trade Organisation (WTO),
  117–20; Dispute Settlements,
  119–20; GATT, 117–18; unlike
  rights interpretation, 119